EUROPEAN POLITICAL, ECONOMIC, AND SECURITY ISSUES

ENGLISH INDUSTRIES OF THE MIDDLE AGES

European Political, Economic, and Security Issues

Additional books in this series can be found on Nova's website under the Series tab.

Additional e-books in this series can be found on Nova's website under the eBooks tab.

European Political, Economic, and Security Issues

English Industries of the Middle Ages

L. F. Salzmann

snova
New York

Library of Congress Cataloging-in-Publication Data

ISBN: 978-1-53613-604-3

Published by Nova Science Publishers, Inc. † New York

CONTENTS

PREFACE*

The title of this book indicates at once its aim and its limitations. It makes no presence to be a complete history of the early industrial life of England, but at the same time it does claim to be an introduction to the study of that subject. It is my hope, and indeed my belief, that from it the general reader, equipped with interest in the history of his country rather than with technical knowledge, will obtain something more than a bare outline of industrial conditions in pre-Elizabethan days. The student who is anxious to go more deeply into the subjects here treated may use this book as a road map and the footnotes as finger-posts to guide him to the heights of completer knowledge.

From the nature of my subject it was inevitable that the book should be full of technicalities, figures, and statistics, but it has been my endeavour to render the technicalities intelligible, and to prevent the significance of the statistics being obscured by an excess of detail. The scheme which I have adopted is to treat the leading medieval industries one by one, showing as far as possible their chief centres, their chronological development, the conditions and the methods of working. With the disposal of the finished products through intermediaries, merchants, or shopkeepers, I have not concerned myself, deeming such matters rather to belong to the realms of trade and commerce than of industry; and for this same reason, and also because it has been dealt with by other writers, I have not dealt with the great source of England's wealth—wool. Agriculture, also, and fishing I have excluded from my definition of industry. A more culpable omission, which I think calls for a word of explanation, is shown in the case of building. This, however, is not

* This is an edited, reformatted and augmented version of a book originally published in 1913 by L. F. Salzmann B.A. F.S.A., Titled "English Industries of The Middle Ages," London: Constable and Company Ltd.

omitted by an oversight, nor yet through any desire to save myself trouble. I had collected a great mass of material for an intended section on the Building Industry, but after careful consideration I came to the conclusion that the material available was so exceedingly technical, and the obscurity of the details so greatly in excess of their value when elucidated, as to render such a section rather a weariness and a stumbling-block to the student than a help. The subjects treated in the several sections are thoroughly representative, if not completely exhaustive, of English industrial life, and a general survey of the subject is contained in my last chapter, where I have outlined as broadly as possible the general principles that governed the Control of Industry—the typical regulations made by, or for, the craftsmen in the interest of the employer, the workman, or the consumer. This last section might, of course, easily have been extended to cover more pages than this whole volume, but it is questionable whether multiplicity of detail tends to ease of assimilation. A single typical instance of a prevalent custom or regulation is as significant as a list of a dozen local variations, and far easier to remember. A rule is more easily remembered by one example than by a score, and with such a wealth of material as exists the risk of obscurity is greater from amplification than from concentration.

As to defining what is meant by the medieval period, it is not easy to lay down any hard and fast rule, for the change from old methods or conditions to new, which practically constitutes the division between the medieval and the modern periods, occurred at a different date in each industry. The crucial point in gunfounding was the invention of solid boring in the time of Henry VIII.; in the cloth industry it was the introduction of the 'new draperies' by Protestant refugees in the reign of Elizabeth; for iron mining it was the adoption of pit coal for smelting in the seventeenth century; for coal mining, the application of steam power to solve the problems of drainage at great depths early in the eighteenth century. Yet, taking one thing with another, the sixteenth century may be considered to be the period of transition. The rise of the capitalist and the monopolist, the social revolution of the Reformation, with the abolition of the monastic houses and the beginnings of the Poor-Law system constituted a new era for the working classes even when unaccompanied by any startling change in methods or mechanical media. Moreover, from the middle of the sixteenth century documents and records relating to industrial matters become more numerous and more accessible, and this is therefore the usual starting-point for those who write upon these subjects. For these reasons my accounts of the various selected industries will be found to end at such dates within the sixteenth century as have seemed convenient, though I have not slavishly refrained from taking out of the seventeenth century occasional details applicable to the earlier period.

Such, then, are the lines upon which I have built my book. If any critic considers that the subject should have been dealt with on another plan, he is at liberty to prove his contention by so treating it himself.

As to the sources from which my information is taken: I believe that every statement will be found to be buttressed by at least one reference, and I may add that the reference is invariably to the actual source from which I obtained my information. Of printed sources much the most valuable have been the series of articles on local industries printed in the Victoria County Histories, those on mining and kindred subjects by Mr. C. H. Vellacott being of exceptional importance. In very few cases have I found any published history of any industry dealing at all fully with the early period: the one conspicuous exception was Mr. G. Randall Lewis's book on The Stannaries, second to which may be put Mr. Galloway's Annals of Coal Mining. The various volumes of municipal records published by, or with the consent of, the public-spirited authorities of some of our ancient boroughs, notably those of Norwich, Bristol, Coventry, and Leicester, have been of great value to me, as have Mr. Riley's Memorials of London and his editions of the Liber Albus and Liber Custumarum. To such other printed works as I have drawn upon, acknowledgment is made in the footnotes, but so far as possible I have made use of unpublished manuscript material at the British Museum and still more at the Record Office. Needless to say, I collected far more material than it was possible to use, and I can only hope that my selection has been wise, as it certainly was careful, and that I have not overlooked or omitted any evidence of essential importance. It had originally been my intention to compile a series of transcripts of industrial records on lines similar to the Documents relatifs à l'Industrie of M. Fagniez, but the enormous mass of material available for such a work, coupled with the fact that in England such original research has to be carried out at the sole expense of the unfortunate researcher, put an end to the project, and deprived this work of what would have been a valuable, if formidable, companion volume.

Chapter 1

Mining—Coal

Coal is so intimately connected with all that is essentially modern—machinery, steam, and the black pall that overhangs our great towns and manufacturing districts—that it comes almost as a surprise to find it in use in Britain at the beginning of the Christian era. Yet excavation has proved beyond all doubt that coal was used by the Romans, ashes and stores of the unburnt mineral being found all along the Wall, at Lanchester and Ebchester in Durham, [1] at Wroxeter [2] in Shropshire and elsewhere. For the most part it appears to have been used for working iron, but it was possibly also used for heating hypocausts, and there seems good reason to believe that it formed the fuel of the sacred fire in the temple of Minerva at Bath, as Solinus, writing about the end of the third century, comments on the 'stony balls' which were left as ashes by this sacred fire [3]. That such coal as was used by the Romans was obtained from outcrops, where the seams came to the surface, is more than probable. There appears to be no certain evidence of any regular mining at this period.

With the departure of the Romans from Britain coal went out of use, and no trace of its employment can be found prior to the Norman Conquest, or indeed for more than a century after that date. It was not until quite the end of the twelfth century that coal was rediscovered, and the history of its use in England may be said for all practical purposes to begin with the reign of Henry III. (1216). In the 'Boldon Book' [4] survey of the see of Durham, compiled in 1183, there are several references to smiths who were bound to make ploughshares and to 'find the coal' therefor, but unfortunately the Latin word invenire bears the same double meaning as its English equivalent 'to find,' and may imply either discovery or simple provision. In view of the fact that the word used for coal (carbonem) in this passage is unqualified, and that carbo, as also the English 'cole,' practically always implies charcoal, it would be unsafe to conclude that mineral coal is here referred to. The latter is almost invariably given a distinguishing adjective, appearing as earth coal, subterranean coal, stone coal, quarry coal, etc., but far most frequently as 'sea coal.' The origin of this term may perhaps be indicated by a passage in a sixteenth-century account of the salt works in the county of Durham: [5] 'As the tide comes in it bringeth a small wash sea coal which is employed to the making of salt and the fuel of the poor fisher towns adjoining.' It is most probable that the first coal used was that thus washed up by the sea and such as could be quarried from the face of the cliffs where the seams were exposed by the action of the waves. The term was next applied, for convenience, to similar coal obtained inland, and as an export trade grew up it acquired the secondary significance of sea-borne coal.

No references to purchases of sea coal occur in the Pipe Rolls of Henry II., nor, so far as I am aware, in those of Richard I. and John, but it would seem that its existence was known before the end of the twelfth century, as Alexander Neckam in his treatise, De Naturis Rerum, [6] has a curious and puzzling section, 'De Carbone,' at the beginning of his discourse on minerals, parts of which seem applicable to sea coal, though other parts appear to refer to charcoal. So far as can be gathered, he considered sea coal to be charcoal found in the earth; he comments on the extreme durability of coal and its resistance to the effects of wet and the lapse of time, and makes the interesting statement that when men were setting up boundary stones they dug in below them a quantity of coal, and that in the event of a dispute as to the position of the stone in later years the presence of this coal was the determining factor. Whether there is any corroborative evidence of this alleged custom I have not been able to ascertain, but it is at least a proof that mineral coal was known, though evidently not extensively used for fuel at this period. Coal was apparently worked in Scotland about 1200, [7] and it would seem that about a quarter of a century later it was being imported into London, as a mention of Sea Coal Lane, just outside the walls of the city, near Ludgate, occurs in 1228 [8]. As property in this lane belonged to William 'de Plessetis,' it is probable that the coal was brought from Plessey, near Blyth, in which neighbourhood the monks of Newminster were given the right to take coal along the shore about 1236 [9]. The monks also obtained leave from Nicholas de Aketon about the same time to take sea coals in his wood of Middlewood for use at their forge of Stretton, near Alnwick. It may be remarked that at this time, and for the greater part of the next three centuries, the use of coal was restricted to iron-working and lime-burning, the absence of chimneys rendering it unsuitable for fuel in ordinary living rooms. So particularly was it associated with lime-burning that we find Sea Coal Lane also known as Lime-burners Lane, and references in building accounts to purchases of sea coal for the burning of lime are innumerable.

It is in 1243 that we get our first dated reference to an actual coal working. In that year Ralf, son of Roger Wlger, was recorded to have been drowned 'in a delf of sea coals' (in fossato carbonum maris) [10]. The use of the word fossatum is interesting, as clearly indicating an 'open cast working,' that is to say, a comparatively shallow trench carried along the seam where it comes close to the surface, a step intermediate between the mere quarrying of outcrop and the sinking of regular pits. An indication of the spread of coal mining is to be found in one of the articles of inquiry for the Forest Assize of 1244, which relates to 'sea coal found within the forest, and whether any one has taken money for the digging of the same' [11]. It is probable that special reference was intended to the Forest of Dean, coal being worked about this time at Blakeney, Stainton, and Abinghall; from the last named place a penny on every horse-load of coal was paid to the Constable of St. Briavels, as warden of the Forest [12]. By 1255 the issues of the Forest of Dean included payments for digging sea coals, and customs on all sea coal brought down the Severn [13]. Some of this latter may have been quarried in Shropshire, as about 1260 Walter de Clifford licensed Sir John de Halston to dig for coals in the forest of Clee, [14] and there are other indications of the early exploitation of the Shropshire coal-field. The Midland field of Derbyshire and Notts was also working, coal being got in Duffield Frith in 1257, [15] the year in which Queen Eleanor was driven from Nottingham Castle by the unpleasant fumes of the sea coal used in the busy town below, [16] a singularly early instance of the smoke nuisance which we are apt to consider a modern evil. Half a century later, in 1307, the growing use of coal by lime-burners in London became so great a nuisance that its use was rigorously prohibited, but whether successfully may be questioned [17].

By the end of the thirteenth century it would seem that practically all the English coal-fields were being worked to some extent. In Northumberland so numerous were the diggings round Newcastle that it was dangerous to approach the town in the dark, and the monks of Tynemouth also were making good use of their mineral wealth; [18] in Yorkshire coal was being got at Shippen at least as early as 1262, [19] and in Warwickshire and at Chilvers Coton in 1275 [20]. The small Somerset field near Stratton on Fosse and the Staffordshire coal measures may be possible exceptions, but in the latter county coal was dug at Bradley in 1315 and at Amblecote during the reign of Edward III [21]. The diggings were still for the most part open-cast works, but pits were beginning to come in. These 'bell pits,' of which numbers remained until recently in the neighbourhood of Leeds, [22] at Oldham in Lancashire, [23] and elsewhere, were narrow shafts sunk down to the coal and then enlarged at the bottom, and widened as far as was safe—and sometimes farther, if we may judge from a number of instances in Derbyshire in which miners were killed by the fall of their pits [24]. When as much coal as could safely be removed had been obtained, the pit was abandoned and a fresh pit sunk as near to it as possible. As a rule the old pit had to be filled up, and at Nuneaton we find this very properly enforced by the bailiff in 1343, [25] and at later dates. Open coal delfs were a source of considerable danger to men and animals, especially when water had accumulated in them, and a number of cattle were drowned at Morley in Derbyshire in 1372, [26] while it was probably in an abandoned working at Wingerworth that a beggar woman, Maud Webster, was killed in 1313 by a mass of soil falling on her as she was picking up coal [27]. From the pits the coal was raised in corves, or large baskets, and as early as 1291 we have a case of a man being killed at Denby in a 'colpyt' by one of these loaded corves falling upon his head [28].

A case of some interest is recorded in Derbyshire in 1322, when Emma, daughter of William Culhare, while drawing water from the 'colepyt' at Morley was killed by 'le Damp,' i.e., choke damp [29]. This is one of the very few early references to choke damp, or 'stithe,' as it was often called, and the case is also interesting because, as water from a coal pit could hardly be good for either drinking or washing purposes, she must have been engaged in draining the pit, and this suggests a pit of rather exceptional dimensions. A more certain indication of a considerable depth having been attained is given forty years later in the case of another pit at Morley Park, said to have been drowned, or flooded, 'for lack of a gutter' [30]. This may only refer to a surface drain, but there is abundant proof that regular drainage by watergates, soughs, or adits had already come into use, and that coal-mining had reached the 'pit and adit' stage. In this system of working, the water, always the most troublesome enemy of the miner, was drawn off by a subterranean drain leading from the bottom of the pit. It need hardly be pointed out that the system was only practicable on fairly high ground, where the bottom of the pit was above the level of free drainage: in such a case a horizontal gallery, or adit, could be driven from a suitable point on the face of the hill slightly below the bottom of the pit to strike the latter, and a wooden sough, [31] or drain, of which the sections were known in Warwickshire as 'dearns,' could be laid to carry the water from the pit to a convenient point of discharge. In 1354 the monks of Durham, when obtaining a lease of coal mines in Ferry, had leave to place pits and watergates where suitable, [32] and ten years later a lease of a mine at Gateshead stipulated for provision of timber for the pits and water-gate [33]. During the next century a certain number of pits were sunk in lower ground, or to a greater depth, below the level of free drainage, and in 1486 we find the monks of Finchale, active exploiters of the northern coal measures, erecting a pump worked by horse power at Moorhouse, [34] but it is not until the second half of the sixteenth century, nearly at the end of the medieval period, that we find such pumps, 'gins,' or baling engines, and similar machines in common use.

Piecing together information afforded by scattered entries, we can obtain some idea of the working of a coal pit about the end of the fifteenth century. After the overseer, or a body of miners, had inspected the ground and chosen a likely place, a space was marked out, and a small sum distributed among the workers as earnest money. The pit was then sunk at such charge as might be agreed upon: at Heworth in 1376 the charge was six shillings the fathom, [35] at Griff in 1603 six shillings the ell [36]. A small 'reward' was paid when the vein of coal was struck, the pit was then cleaned up and timbered, and a water-gate or adit driven to afford drainage and ventilation. Over the mouth of the pit was erected a thatched 'hovel' with wattled sides to keep the wind and rain from the pit, and in this was a windlass for raising the corves. The workmen consisted of hewers, who cut the coal, and bearers who carried it to the bottom of the pit and filled the corves: they were under the control of the 'viewer,' whose duty it was 'to see under the ground that the work was orderly wrought,' and the 'overman,' who had 'to see such work as come up at every pit to be for the coal owner's profit' [37]. Their wages do not appear to have been much, if at all, above those of the ordinary labourer or unskilled artisan. Owing no doubt to the comparatively late rise of the industry and the simplicity of the work, no refining or skilled manipulation being required as in the case of metallic ores, the coal miners never acquired the privileged position of the 'free miners' of Dean, Derbyshire, Cumberland, and Cornwall [38]. The work was not attractive, and the supply of labour seems occasionally to have run dry. So much was this the case after the Black Death in 1350 and the second epidemic of 1366 that the lessees of the great mines at Whickham and Gateshead had to resort to forced labour, and obtained leave to impress workmen [39]. Much later, about 1580, the Winlaton pits were hampered by lack of workmen and the owners, having sent into Scotland for more hands with little success, had to hire women and even then were short-handed, to say nothing of being troubled with incompetent men who for their negligence and false work had to be 'laid in the stocks,' and even 'expulsed oute of their worke' [40].

The question of mineral rights as regards coal is complicated by the variety of local customs. In some cases, as at Bolsover, [41] the manorial tenants had the right to dig sea coal in the waste and forest land for their own use; but it was probably usual to charge a fee for licence to dig, and this was clearly the practice at Wakefield [42]. So far as copyhold lands were concerned the lord of the manor, or his farmer, appears as a rule to have had the power to dig without paying the tenant compensation. This was certainly being done at Houghton, in Yorkshire, and in the adjacent manor of Kipax in 1578, and the undoubted injury to the copyholders was held to be counterbalanced by the advantage to the neighborhood of a cheap supply of coal [43]. The uncertainty of the law and the conflicting claims of ground landlords, tenants, and prospectors led to a plentiful crop of legal actions. For the most part these were actions for trespass in digging coal without leave, occasionally complicated by counter appeals [44]. In the first half of the sixteenth century, for instance, Nicholas Strelley, being impleaded for trespass by Sir John Willoughby, set forth that he had a pit in Strelley from which he obtained much coal, to the advantage of the neighbourhood and of 'the schyres of Leicestre and Lincoln, being very baren and scarce contres of all maner of fuell'; and no doubt, though he omitted to say so, to his own advantage; now, owing to the deepness of the mine and the amount of water, the old pit could only be worked if a sough or drain were constructed at an unreasonable expense; he had therefore dug a fresh pit on the borders of Strelly close to Sir John's manor of Wollaton, purposing to use an old sough running through Sir John's ground. Sir John had promptly blocked the sough with a 'counter-mure' and brought actions for trespass, and Nicholas Strelley, much aggrieved, invoked the aid of the Star Chamber [45]. The same court was also invoked a few years later by William Bolles, who complained that by the procurement of Sir William Hussey certain persons came to Newthorpe Mere in Gresley and 'most cruelly and maliciously cutt in peaces brake and caste downe dyvers frames of tymbre made upon and in one pitte made and sonken to gett cooles, and cutt in peaces dyvers greate ropes loomes and tooles apperteyninge to the said woorke at the said pitte,' the offenders being unidentified as the outrage took place 'in the night tyme when every good trew and faithful subjecte ought to take their reste' [46].

Presuming an undisputed title, the owner of coal measures could exploit them in a variety of ways. He might work them himself; the outlay would be small, provided extensive drainage operations were not required, for wages, as we have said, were low and the equipment of the mine, consisting of a few picks, iron bars or wedges, wooden shovels shod with iron and baskets, buckets, and ropes, inexpensive, and there was a steady sale for the coal, though the price of coal varied so greatly and was so much affected by cost of carriage that it is not possible to give even an approximate average value for the medieval period; the question being further complicated by the extraordinary variety of measure employed. Coal is quoted in terms of the 'hundredweight,' the 'quarter' (valued at Colchester in 1296 at 6d.), [47] the 'seam' (or horse-load), the 'load,' which may be either horse or wain load, the 'scope,' which appears to be equivalent to the 'corf,' or basket, the 'roke' or 'rowe,' the 'rod' or 'perch' (a measure apparently peculiar to Warwickshire), [48] the 'butress' and the 'three-quarters' (of a buttress), and most commonly in the Tyne district by the 'fother,' 'chalder,' or 'chaldron' and 'ten,' and also by the 'keel' or barge load. Where the owner did not work the coals himself he could either issue annual licences to dig coal or lease the mines for a term of years [49]. The earliest leases give a vague general permission to dig coal wherever found within the lands in question, but it soon became usual to limit the output either by fixing the maximum amount to be taken in one day, or more usually in early leases by restricting the number of workmen to be employed. In 1326 Hugh of Scheynton granted to Adam Peyeson land at Benthall with all quarries of sea coal, employing four labourers to dig the same, and as many as he chose to carry the coals to the Severn [50]. Slightly before this date we find that payment was made at Belper according to the number of picks employed, the royalty on one pick in 1315 being over £4 [51]. In 1380 the prior of Beauvale in leasing a mine of sea coal at Newthorpe to Robert Pascayl and seven other partners, [52] stipulated that they should have only got two men in the pit, a viewer (servaunt de south la terre), and three men above ground. The lessees of a pit at Trillesden in 1447 were 'to work and win coal every day overable [i.e., working day] with three picks and ilk pick to win every day 60 scopes,' [53] and at Nuneaton, in 1553, the lessees were not to employ more than six workmen at the time [54]. In this latter case there was a further stipulation that the pits when exhausted should be filled up with 'yearthe and slecke,' while at Trillesden the pit was to be worked workmanlike and the miners were to 'save the field standing,' pointing to a fairly elaborate system of galleries and pillars liable to subsidence if not properly planned [55]. But the most important lease was that of five mines in Whickham, made in 1356 by Bishop Hatfield of Durham to Sir Thomas Gray and the Rector of Whickham for the enormous rent of 500 marks (£333, 6s.

8d.) [56]. In this case the lessees were limited to one keel (about twenty tons) daily from each mine; but on the other hand the bishop agreed never to take their workmen away, and not to open any fresh pits in the district, and not to sell the coal from his existing pits at Gateshead to ships. A century later Sir William Eure leased some of the most important Durham coal mines, his daily output being restricted to 340 corves at Raly, 300 at Toftes, 600 at Hartkeld, and 20 at any other mines, with the right of making up from one mine any deficiency in another, and also of making up any deficiency caused by delays due to 'styth' or choke-damp, which appears to have been so troublesome in the hot season as to cause a complete suspension of work. Under this lease Sir William obtained at Raly in one week of 1460, some 1800 corves, each of 2½ bushels, making rather over 140 chalders, paying 5d. a day to each of the three hewers, the three barrowmen, who brought the coal to the foot of the shaft, and the four drawers who raised and banked it [57].

In the Whickham lease of 1356 it will be noticed that the bishop undertook not to allow coals from his own pits to be exported by sea. The sea-borne trade in coals from Newcastle and the Tyne was obtaining considerable dimensions; ten years later, in 1366, a large purchase of coal was made at Winlaton for the king's works at Windsor. The sheriff of Northumberland accounted for £165, 5s. 2d. expended on the purchase and carriage to London of 576 chalder of coals, reckoning by the 'great hundred' of six score, so that there were actually shipped 676 chalder, but of this 86 chalder had to be written off, partly through some being jettisoned during a sudden storm at sea, and partly because the London chalder was much bigger than that used in Northumberland, the difference amounting to about five per cent [58]. The chalder, or chaldron, seems to have been originally about eighteen to twenty hundredweight, and from early times twenty of these made the load of a keel, or coal barge, but in order to evade the export duty of 2d. on every keel, or at least to compensate for it, it became the practice to build keels of twenty-two or twenty-three chalder burden. This was forbidden in 1385, [59] but the prohibition being evaded, an Act was passed in 1421 [60] by which the actual capacity of each keel had to be marked upon it. This in turn was evaded by a rapid increase in the size of the chalder, until by the time of Elizabeth it had doubled its original weight, and the 'ten' (chalder) was the equivalent of the keel of twenty tons [61]. Returning to the fourteenth century, the customs accounts of the port of Newcastle [62] show that between Michaelmas 1377 and Michaelmas 1378 as much as 7338 chalder of coal, valued at 2s. the chalder, was exported to foreign countries. For the most part this went to the Low Countries—Sluys, Bremerhaven, Flushing, and Dunkirk being amongst the ports mentioned, though in a number of cases ships of 'Lumbardye' occur, the average quantity taken by each vessel being a little less than fifty chalder. Of the home trade for this period no record is obtainable, and it is not until the time of Elizabeth that we can compare the exports to home and foreign ports. For the seven years 1591-7, the amount sent abroad was 95,558 chalder, rising from 10,000 in 1591 to 18,000 in 1593, and then falling gradually back to 10,000, while the home trade amounted to 418,200 chalder, increasing steadily from 45,700 up to over 70,000 [63]. The supremacy of Newcastle is shown by a comparison of the amounts of coal exported to foreign countries from the chief English ports in 1592 [64]. Newcastle comes first with 12,635 chalder, then Bristol with 580, Wales with 464, and Liverpool with 448.

The expansion of the home trade noticed in the returns for 1591-7 is borne out by an abundance of corroborative evidence, and may be largely attributed to the great increase at this period in the use of chimneys. Practically the chimney was an Elizabethan invention so far as the smaller houses were concerned, and 'the multitude of chimnies lately erected' was one of the changes most remarked upon by Harrison's old friends at the time that he wrote his Description of England, published in 1577. The reign of Elizabeth, therefore, when the rapid increase in the demand for house coal, coupled with a rise in the price, resulted in a rapid expansion of the industry in all parts of the country, marks the end of the medieval period of coal mining and the initiation of a new epoch with which we are not concerned.

Chapter 2

MINING—IRON

Iron has been worked in Britain from the earliest historical times, and flint implements have been found at Stainton-in-Furness and at Battle in Sussex in positions suggesting that ironworks existed in those places at the end of the Stone Age [65]. Julius Caesar relates that iron was produced along the coast of Britain, but only in small quantities, its rarity causing it to be considered as a precious metal, so that iron bars were current among the natives as money. The coming of the Romans soon changed this. They were not slow to see the value of the island's mineral wealth and to turn it to account. Ironworks sprang up all over the country: at Maresfield in Sussex they were apparently in full swing by the time of Vespasian (died A.D. 79), and in the neighbourhood of Battle fifty years later. Even more important were the workings in the West, on the banks of the Wye and in the Forest of Dean. Near Coleford have been found remains of Roman mines with shallow shafts and adits, while round Whitchurch, Goodrich, and Redbrook are enormous deposits of 'cinders,' or slag, dating from the same period [66]. Ariconium, near Ross, was a city of smiths and forgemen; and Bath (Aquae Sulis) is often said to have had a 'collegium fabricensium,' or gild of smiths, as one of its members, Julius Vitalis, armourer of the 20th Legion, dying after nine years' service, was given a public funeral here by his gild; but it seems more probable that the seat of the gild was at Chester, and that Julius had come to Bath for his health [67].

It is a most remarkable fact that although abundant circumstantial evidence of the Roman exploitation of British iron exists in the shape of coins and other relics found upon the site of the works, there is practically no trace of any such working during the Saxon period until shortly before the Conquest. The furnaces must have been still in blast when the Saxons landed;

they were a warlike race, possessing a full appreciation of iron and something of the Scandinavian admiration for smithcraft, yet there is hardly a trace of their having worked iron in this country. Few, if any, objects definitely assignable to this period have been found upon the site of iron works, and documentary evidence is almost non-existent. There is a charter of Oswy, King of Kent, given in 689, by which he grants to the abbey of St. Peter of Canterbury land at Liminge 'in which there is known to be a mine of iron'; [68] and there is the legend that about 700 A.D. Alcester, in Warwickshire, was the centre of busy ironworks, peopled with smiths, who, for their hardness of heart in refusing to listen to St. Egwin, and endeavoring to drown his voice by beating on their anvils, were swallowed up by the earth; [69] but the rest is silence, until we come to the time of Edward the Confessor. The Domesday Survey shows that in the time of the Confessor, Gloucester rendered as part of its farm 36 dicres of iron, probably in the form of horseshoes, and 100 rods suitable for making bolts for the king's ships, [70] while from Pucklechurch in the same country came yearly 90 'blooms' of iron. [71] The same Survey mentions that there were six smiths in Hereford, each of whom had yearly to make for the king 120 horseshoes, and it also refers to iron mines on the borders of Cheshire, in Sussex and elsewhere.

During the twelfth century the industry appears to have expanded. In the North, at Egremont, we read of the grant of an iron mine to the monks of St. Bees, [72] and at Denby a similar grant was made about 1180 by William FitzOsbert to the abbey of Byland [73]. In Derbyshire, towards the end of the century, Sir Walter de Abbetoft gave to the monks of Louth Park wood at Birley in Brampton and two smithies, namely one bloomery and one forge, with the right to take beech and elm for fuel [74]. But it was in the south-west that the greatest development took place. During the whole of this century the Forest of Dean was the centre of the iron industry, and played the part that Birmingham has played in more recent times. All through the reign of Henry II. the accounts of the sheriffs of Gloucester [75] tell of a constant output of iron, both rough and manufactured, iron bars, nails, pickaxes, and hammers sent to Woodstock, Winchester, and Brill, where the king was carrying out extensive building operations, horseshoes supplied to the army, arrows and other warlike materials despatched to France, spades, pickaxes, and other miners' tools provided for the Irish expedition of 1172, iron bought for the Crusade which Henry projected, but did not live to perform, and 50,000 horseshoes made for the actual Crusade of Richard I. Throughout the thirteenth century the Forest of Dean retained its practical monopoly of the English iron trade, so far at least as the southern counties were concerned, and during the whole of that time members of the family of Malemort were employed at a forge near the castle of St. Briavels turning out enormous stores of bolts for cross-bows and other war material [76]. But a rival was now growing up in the Weald of Sussex and Kent. As early as 1254 the sheriff of Sussex had been called upon to provide 30,000 horseshoes and 60,000 nails, presumably of local manufacture, [77] and in 1275 Master Henry of Lewes, who had been the king's chief smith for the past twenty years, [78] purchased 406 iron rods (kiville) 'in the Weald' for £16, 17s. 11d., [79] while a year or two later he obtained another 75 rods from the same source and paid £4, 3s. 4d. 'to a certain smith in the Weald for 100 iron rods' [80].

The Wealden works had the advantage, a great advantage in the case of so heavy a material as iron, of nearness to London, and soon obtained a footing in the London markets with the imported Spanish iron at the expense of Gloucestershire, which at the beginning of the reign of Henry III. had been sending its iron to Westminster and into Sussex [81]. It must not be imagined that the northern counties were neglecting their mineral wealth all this time; they were on the contrary very active, and were exploiting their iron with vigour and success. On the lands of Peter de Brus in Cleveland in 1271 there were five small forges each valued at 10s., and two larger worth £4 each: [82] these sums may not sound very imposing, but it must be borne in mind that the best land in that district was then worth only 1s. an acre. Twenty years later the forges belonging to Furness Abbey yielded a profit of £6, 13s. 4d., as compared with a profit on flocks and herds of only £3, 11s. 3d., and it is probable that the Abbey had at least forty forges then working on their lands [83]. The great quantity of iron obtained at Furness, also, formed the most valuable part of the booty carried off by the Scots in their raid in 1316 [84]. But the large production of iron in the northern counties was absorbed by their own local requirements, and this was still more the case with the smaller quantities smelted in Northampton shire and Rutland. Derbyshire must have been another important centre, for as early as 1257 four or five forges in the Belper ward of Duffield Frith were yielding about £10 each yearly, and in 1314 two forges in Belper accounted for £63, 6s. 8d. in thirty-four weeks, and there was a third, yielding nearly £7, 10s. for only eleven weeks' work, [85] but there is nothing to show that Derbyshire iron was ever sent south, and from the middle of the fourteenth century such English iron as was used in London was almost entirely drawn from the Weald.

In order to understand how Sussex and Kent, where no iron has been worked for the last hundred years, came to be the centres of a great iron industry in medieval times, it must be borne in mind that charcoal was the only fuel used for iron working [86] until Dud Dudley discovered a method of using pit coal, about 1620, a date which may be considered to mark the end of the medieval period in iron mining. The earliest and most primitive method of smelting iron was by setting a hearth of wood and charcoal on a wind-swept hill or in some other draughty position, heaping upon it alternate layers of ore and charcoal, and covering the whole with clay, to retain the heat, leaving vents at the base for the wind to enter and the iron to come out [87]. A slight advance on this substituted a short cylindrical furnace of stone for the containing layer of clay, and an ingenious device for increasing the draught was used by the Romans at Lanchester, in Durham, where two narrow tunnels were made on the side of a hill, with wide mouths facing to the west, the quarter from which the wind blows most frequently in this valley, tapering to a narrow bore at the hearth [88]. Even under the most favourable conditions such a furnace would reduce a very small percentage of the ore to metal, [89] and the use of an auxiliary blast, produced by bellows, must have been resorted to at a quite early date. Prior to the fifteenth century such bellows were almost invariably worked by hand, or rather by foot, for the blowers stood upon the bellows, holding on to a bar, but during the fifteenth century water power was introduced in many parts of the country, and the bellows were driven by water-wheels. Such was apparently the case in Weardale in 1408, [90] probably in the Forest of Dean about the same date, and clearly in Derbyshire by the end of the century [91].

In several early charters granting mineral rights to Furness Abbey, mention is made of the privilege of using water from the grantor's streams; but where particulars are given, as in the case of the charter of Hugh de Moresby made in 1270, the water is always stated to be for the washing of the ore, and not for power [92]. The ore, or 'mine,' to use the more common medieval term, was sometimes dug on the 'open-cast' system, but more usually by a series of bell or beehive pits [93]. It was then roughly cleansed by washing on a coarse sieve, and was next subjected to a preliminary burning, or 'elyng,' [94] as it was termed at the Tudeley forge in the fourteenth century [95]. The burnt ore was then broken and carried to the furnace. In the sixteenth century this was a building in the shape of a truncated cone, about twenty-four feet in diameter, and not more than thirty feet high, in the base of which was a cupped, or bowl-shaped, hearth of sandstone, and such we may assume the earlier furnaces also to have been. Alternate charges of mine and charcoal were fed into the furnace from the top, the iron settling down into the bowl of the hearth, from which it was taken as a lump or 'bloom.' From the sixteenth century, when by the use of a more powerful blast a higher temperature was obtainable and cast iron was produced, the molten iron was drawn off from time to time through a vent at the bottom of the hearth into a bed of sand. In Sussex and Gloucestershire it seems to have been usual to form in the sand one large oblong depression in the direct course of the flow of the iron with a number of smaller depressions at right angles to the first, the large mass of iron thus moulded being known as a 'sow,' and the smaller blocks as 'pigs.'

There were in the earlier periods of the industry a very large number of smelting hearths, consisting practically of an ordinary blacksmith's forge with a cup-shaped hearth, or crucible, in the bottom of which the imperfectly molten iron accumulated. Such were the itinerant forges (fabricae errantes) in the Forest of Dean, of which there were as many as sixty in blast at the end of the thirteenth century [96]. The buildings attached to such a forge would naturally be merely temporary sheds, such as were referred to by the Earl of Richmond in 1281, when he gave leave to the monks of Jervaux to cut wood in his forest to smelt iron and to make two small sheds (logias) 'without nail, bolt, or wall,' so that if the smelters moved to another place (as these itinerant forges did when the ore or the fuel became exhausted) they should pull down the sheds and erect others [97]. In this instance the grant of two sheds may imply two smelting-houses, but it seems more probable that one was the 'bloomery,' or smelting forge, and the other the smithy, which invariably accompanied the bloomery [98]. With this simple type of forge the product was a lump of malleable iron, which was purified by hammering and worked up at the smithy, but the pig iron produced by the larger high blast furnace required more elaborate treatment. The sow was carried from the furnace to the forge, 'finery' or 'stryngheard,' where it was heated on an open hearth and reduced by the sledge, or by the water-hammer [99] when available, to a large ingot or 'bloom' [100]. The latter was, as a rule, reheated, divided and worked into bars, the completion of which was usually carried out in the seventeenth century at a third hearth, the 'chafery,' but this appears to have been an elaboration of post-medieval date. The sows naturally varied in size according to the capacity of the furnace, and this, it may be observed, was much greater at the end of a 'blowing' than at the beginning, owing to the fire eating away the hearth, especially if too large a proportion of intractable 'hot' ore were used; [101] but the blooms were made of standard weight. At the same time the weight of the bloom, though constant in any given district, varied in different parts of the country. In Weardale it seems to have been about two hundredweight, being composed of fifteen stones, each of thirteen pounds; [102] and in Furness it was about the same weight, but contained fourteen stones of fourteen pounds [103]. On the other hand, we find blooms selling at the Kentish ironworks of Tudeley for 3s. 4d. in the reign of Edward III., [104] when iron bought for repairs to Leeds Castle cost about 7s. the hundredweight, [105] which, allowing for cost of carriage, agrees fairly well with the three quarters of a hundredweight attributed to the Sussex bloom in the seventeenth century [106]. As regards the price of iron, it was always high during the medieval period, but naturally varied with conditions of demand and supply, cost of carriage, and the quality of the iron. To take a late instance: in Staffordshire in 1583, 'coldshear,' or brittle iron, fetched only £9 the ton when tough iron fetched £12 [107]. In Sussex [108] in 1539 iron sold on the spot for from £5 to £7 the ton, allowing a profit of 20s. the ton, and ten years later £8 at the forge and about £9, 5s. in London, the cost of carriage to London being 9s. the ton [109].

The number of workmen employed at the different works naturally varied, but the surveyor of the iron mills in Ashdown Forest in 1539 laid down the rule: [110] 'That to melt the sowes in ij forges or fynories there must be iiij persones, and at the forge to melt the blomes there must be ij persones. So are there at every forge ij persones wherof the oone holdeth the work at the hamo r and the second kepeth the work hot. M d that oone man cannot kepe the hamo r bicause the work must be kept in such hete that they may not shifte handes.'

At the Bedburn forge in 1408, [111] there were a 'blomer' or 'smythman,' a smith and a foreman, as well as a 'colier' or charcoal burner. The blomer was paid 6d. for every bloom smelted, of which the average production was six in a week, the largest output recorded in any week being ten blooms. For working up the bloom at the forge, the smith received 6d. and an extra penny for cutting it up into bars, while the foreman, who in spite of his name does not seem to have had any staff of workmen under him, received 2d. a bloom when he assisted at the smelting, and 3d. at the reworking. Such additional labour as was required was supplied by the wives of the smith and foreman, who did odd jobs, breaking up the ore, attending to the bellows, or helping their husbands, earning wages paid at first on a vague but rather high scale, but falling afterwards to the settled rate of a halfpenny a bloom. An allowance of one penny a week was made for ale for the workmen; and a similar munificent allowance was made 'for drink for the four blowers' at Tudeley in 1353 [112]. At this Tudeley forge in 1333, the workmen were paid in kind, receiving every seventh bloom, [113] a payment roughly equivalent to 6d. a bloom, but by 1353 this system had been dropped, and they were paid from 7½d. to 9½d. a bloom. In addition to the 'seventh bloom,' we find mention in 1333 of a customary payment to the 'Forblouweris' [114] of 2¼d. a bloom, and in the 1353 account we find 'rewards' paid to the master blower and three other blowers; no other workmen are mentioned by name, and as the whole process of making the blooms is here referred to as 'blowyng' we may probably assume that the staff of these Kentish works consisted of four men. The Sussex iron mills at Sheffield in Fletching in 1549 employed one hammerman and his assistant, [115] two fyners and their two servants, a founder, and a filler, [116] the business of the latter being to keep the furnace charged. Here the founder was paid 8s., and the filler 6s. for each 'foundye,' or working week of six days, and the hammerman and fyners received between them 13s. 4d. a ton, about three tons being produced each 'foundye.'

In addition to the actual ironworkers every forge afforded employment to a number of charcoal- burners and miners. For the most part these latter, as was the case with the coal miners, ranked as ordinary labourers, but in the Forest of Dean they formed a close corporation of 'free miners,' possessing an organisation and privileges of considerable importance and antiquity [117]. So far as can be judged the customs of the free miners were traditional, based on prescription, recognised as early as the time of Henry III. , and officially confirmed by Edward I. By these customs the right of mining was restricted to the free miners' resident within the bounds of the Forest, and they had also control of the export of the iron ore, all persons carrying the same down the Severn being bound to pay dues to the miners under penalty of forfeiture of their boat. The free miners had also the right of digging anywhere within the Forest, except in gardens, orchards, and curtilages; the lord of the soil, who might be the king or a private landowner, being entitled to a share as a member of the fellowship, almost always consisting of four 'verns' or partners. Besides the right thus to open a mine the miners had a claim to access thereto from the highway, and to timber for their works. In return, the king received from every miner who raised three loads of ore in a week one penny, which was collected by the 'gaveller' every Tuesday 'between Mattens and Masse,' and he had also the right to certain quantities of 'law-ore' from the different mines every week, for which the miners were paid at the rate of a penny a load, and if he was working an itinerant forge they were bound to supply ore therefor at the same rate, and finally there was a royal export duty of a halfpenny on every load of ore taken out of the Forest [118].

The right of mining within the forest was restricted, as we have already said, to the resident free miners, and they might only employ the labour of their own family or apprentices. These rights to their mines, or shares therein, were definite, and could be bequeathed by will; and in order to prevent trespass the rule was laid down that no man should start a fresh working near that of another miner 'within so much space that the miner may stand and cast ridding [119] and stones so far from him with a bale, as the manner is.' When disputes arose between the miners, they were settled at their own court, held every three weeks at St. Briavels, under the presidency of the Constable, appeals being made, if necessary, from the normal jury of twelve miners to juries of twenty-four or forty-eight. These Mine Law Courts continued to be held until the latter half of the eighteenth century; but we are not here concerned with their later proceedings and constant endeavours to maintain restrictions which had long passed out of date; endeavours which seem to have resulted chiefly in promoting 'the abominable sin of perjury,' so that it was found necessary to ordain that any miner convicted thereof should be expelled and 'all the working tooles and habitt burned before his face.' What those tools and costume were in the fifteenth century, and until modern times, may be seen on a brass in Newland Church, whereon is depicted a free miner wearing a cap and leather breeches tied below the knee, with a wooden mine-hod slung over his shoulder, carrying a small mattock in his right hand, and holding a candlestick between his teeth [120].

Although not so intimately connected with iron working as the smiths, smelters and miners, the charcoal-burners were auxiliaries without whom the industry could not have existed, and who in turn derived their living largely from that industry. The amount of wood consumed by the iron works was enormous. As an example we may take the case of the two Sussex mills of Sheffield and Worth for 1547-9 [121]. At Sheffield 6300 cords of wood were 'coled' for the furnace, and 6750 cords for the forge; at Worth the amounts were respectively nearly 5900 and 2750 cords; the cords being 125 cubic feet, this represents an expenditure of about 2,175,000 cubic feet of timber for these two works alone in less than two years. Later, in 1580, it was stated that a beech tree of one foot square 'at the stubbe' would make one and a half loads of charcoal, and the ironworks at Monkswood, near Tintern, would require 600 such trees every year, [122] while some thirty years later Norden referred to the fact that there were in Sussex alone about 140 forges using two, three, or four loads of charcoal apiece daily. Acts were passed in 1558, 1581, and 1585 regulating the cutting of wood for furnaces and prohibiting the use of timber trees for charcoal, but they were evaded, and the destruction of trees continued until in the eighteenth century charcoal was supplanted by mineral coal, the first successful use of which for iron smelting, by Dud Dudley in 1620, marks, as we have said, the termination of the medieval period.

Chapter 3

MINING—LEAD AND SILVER

The lead-mining industry in England is important and interesting from its antiquity, the value of its produce, large quantities of silver being obtained from this source during the medieval period, and the organisation of its workers. Although lacking the completeness of organisation which rendered the tinners of Cornwall and Devon almost an independent race, the lead miners of Alston Moor, Derbyshire, and the Mendips, the three great mining camps of England, were more highly organised than the iron miners of Dean, who form the lowest class of privileged 'free miners.'

The lead mines of Britain were worked by the Romans from the earliest days of their occupation of the island, pigs of lead having been found in the Mendips stamped with the titles of Britannicus (A.D. 44-48) and Claudius (A.D. 49) [123]. Mines of this period exist at Shelve and Snailbeach in Shropshire and elsewhere, and smelting-hearths have been found at Minsterley in the same county and at Matlock [124]. Nor was the industry discontinued after the departure of the Romans. Lead mines at Wirksworth in Derbyshire were leased by the Abbess of Repton to a certain Duke Humbert in 835, [125] and a 'leadgedelf' at Penpark Hole in Gloucestershire is mentioned in 882, [126] though that county was not a great centre of lead production at a later date. In the time of Edward the Confessor the Derbyshire mines of Bakewell, Ashford, and Hope yielded £30, besides five wainloads of lead, but in 1086 their yearly value had fallen, for some reason, to £10, 6s. Besides these three mines Domesday Book alludes to others at Wirksworth, Metesford, and Crich [127].

During the twelfth century the output of lead was considerable. The 'mines of Carlisle,' that is to say of Alston Moor, on the borders of

Cumberland, Yorkshire, and Northumberland, occur on the Pipe Roll of 1130, and were farmed during the reign of Henry II [128] at an average rent of £100; during the same reign large quantities of lead from Derbyshire were carried across to Boston and shipped to London and the Continent: the Shropshire mines were also active, one hundred and ten loads of lead being sent down to Amesbury in 1181 alone. King Stephen granted to the Bishop of Durham certain mines in Weardale, probably of silver-bearing lead, as the non-precious minerals already belonged to the bishopric, and during the vacancy of the see of Durham in 1196 considerable issues of silver were accounted for [129]. A similar grant of lead mines in Somerset was made to Bishop Reginald of Bath by Richard I [130]. How soon the three great mining camps acquired their privileges and organisation cannot be definitely stated: some of the regulations seem to have been traditional from very early times, even in the case of the Mendip mines, of which the laws were largely based upon the Derbyshire code. So far as the northern mines are concerned, we find Henry III in 1235 confirming to the miners of Alston the liberties and privileges 'which they used to have' [131].

Of the regulations in force at Alston Moor [132] we have but few details, but of the laws of Derbyshire [133] and the Mendips [134] we have ample information. In each case there was a mine court, known in Derbyshire as the 'berghmote' or 'barmote,' of which the ordinary meetings were held every three weeks and special sessions twice a year, at Easter and Michaelmas. The 'body of the court' consisted of twelve, or in the 'great courts' twenty-four, miners of good standing and the presiding officer was in Derbyshire the barmaster and in Somerset the lead-reeve: at Alston [135] he appears as bailiff, 'king's serjeant,' and steward. Associated with this official was the coroner: [136] the two offices indeed seem to have been combined at Alston during the thirteenth century as in 1279 complaint was made that the coroners of the Scottish king's liberty of Tindale (that portion of the present county of Northumberland which adjoins Alston Moor) were acting in the mine 'where the serjeant of the mine appointed by the English king ought to exercise the office of coroner in all things': [137] by 1356, however, it was the custom for the Alston miners to elect a coroner separate from the bailiff or king's serjeant [138]. The exact degree of independence possessed by these mine courts is difficult to determine. During eyres in Cumberland it was customary to send special justices to Alston to hold the pleas of the Crown. This was already an old-established custom in 1246, [139] and we find that Robert de Vipont, who about the beginning of the reign of Edward I. had formed a manor out of what had been moor and waste, had usurped the right to try thieves in his manor court, when they ought only to be tried in the mine court. [140] Even in Derbyshire there was a tendency to use the courts of the Duchy of Lancaster instead of, or to overrule, the mine courts, at least in the sixteenth century [141].

By the Derbyshire mine law a small trespass was punishable by a fine of 2d., but if this was not paid at once the fine was doubled each successive day until it reached the sum of 5s. 4d. This same sum of 5s. 4d. (doubled in a similar way up to 100s.) was the fine for bloodshed, or for the offence of encroaching upon another man's claim underground. For a thrice-repeated theft of ore the offender's hand was pinned with a knife to the uprights of his windlass, and if he succeeded in getting free he had to forswear the mine for ever. A similarly savage and primitive measure of justice was meted out to the Mendip miner who stole lead worth 13½d.: his property was forfeited, and the bailiff was to bring him 'where hys howse or wore [i.e., ore] hys, hys work and towlls with all instruments belongyng to that occupacyon and then put hym in hys howss or working place and set fyer yn all together about hym—banyshe hym from that occupacyon for ever by fore the face of all the myners there.' Both methods of punishment are clearly of early origin, and it seems probable that they originally involved the death of the thief, though a later and more humane generation connived at his escape while retaining the ancient form of punishment. If the burnt thief did not dread the fire, but returned and stole again, he was handed over to the sheriff's officers and committed to prison, being no longer one of the privileged community. It is worth noting that the great mining camp on the borders of Cornwall and Devon, though not apparently possessing any mine court, had, as we might expect, certain control over the excesses of the miners, as in

1302 there was made 'a pit in the mine by way of prison to frighten (ad terrorem) evildoers and bad workmen' [142]. The Devon miner, as we have just said, had no code of laws or privileges; at Alston the code applied only to the miners actually living in the collection of 'shiels,' or huts on the Moor; in Derbyshire the full system of regulations was confined to the royal 'field,' though a few private owners of mining fields established barmotes on similar lines; [143] but the customs of the Mendips appear to have applied throughout the district, whoever might be lord of the soil.

By mining law the miner had the right to prospect anywhere except in churchyards, gardens, orchards, and highways; on the Mendips, however, he had first to go through the formality of asking leave of the lord of the soil, or of his lead-reeve, who could not refuse their permission; he might then pitch where he pleased and break ground as he thought best. In Derbyshire, when the prospector had struck a promising 'rake' or vein, he cut a cross in the ground and went to the barmaster, who came and staked out the claim into 'meers,' each being four perches of twenty- four feet: the first two meers were given to the finder, the third to the king, as lord of the soil, and the others to those miners who first demanded them. Within three days the owner of a meer must set up a 'stow,' [144] a wooden frame with two uprights joined by a bar or spindle placed at the top of the shaft, and serving as a windlass. If the claim was not then worked, the barmaster nicked the spindle, and if this were done three times, and the claim was still unworked, it was declared forfeit and granted to the first applicant. The regulations in use on the Mendip field were rather different. There the pitches or claims, instead of being of one standard size, were decided by the throw of the 'hack' or small pick, weighing 3 lbs. 14 oz. 'Every man when he doth begyn hys pyt, otherwyse callyd a grouff, shaull have hys haks throw ij weys after the rake, [145] so that he do stand to the gyrdyl or wast in the gruff'; while this decided the limits of the pitch along the line of the vein the pitcher had always eighteen feet on either side of his 'grooffe or gribbe.' The hack, however, was not thrown unless another party wished to pitch in the neighbourhood; in that case the newcomer, or 'younger pitcher,' could demand that the hack be thrown by the 'elder pitcher' and his partners, 'when they have their chine, rake or course,' that is to say, when they have struck the vein. The lead-reeve then proffered the hack to one of the elder pitchers, and if they failed to throw it within fourteen days the younger pitcher had the throw [146]. The rules for reserving a claim were probably founded on those in use in Derbyshire. 'The first pytcher in any grounde muste make yt perfecte wyth a caddel of tymber and a payre of styllyngs within fowre and twentie howers next after the pyching.' Although this was the strict law, custom seems to have been content with the making of the 'caddel,' some sort of framework of timber, the first day, and to have allowed a month for the 'styllyngs,' or stow. If a claim lay unworked for four weeks, the lead-reeve caused proclamation to be made, and if the old partners did not turn up within fourteen days, it was forfeited.

Besides the right of prospecting where they chose, the miners had right of access to the nearest high-road, and in Derbyshire if this were refused them the barmaster and two assistants might walk abreast with arms stretched out, and so mark out a way direct from the mines to the road, even through growing corn. They were also privileged to take timber from the neighbouring woods for use in the mines, and in Cumberland, where fuel was scarce, they might even prevent the owners of the woods from cutting them until they had obtained a sufficient supply for the furnaces. Their proprietary rights in their mines were recognised, and they could dispose of them, wholly or in part, without licence. They might also take their ore to what 'myndry' they pleased, to be smelted, and the only restriction upon the sale of the ore or lead was that in some places the king, or other lord of the soil, had 'coup,' that is to say pre-emption, the right of buying the ore at the market price before it was offered to any other purchaser, and in 1295 we find the Derbyshire miners paying 4d. a load in respect of 'coup' for licence to sell to whom they pleased [147].

The terms upon which the miners held their mines varied. On private lands, when the owner did not work the mines himself by hired labour, he usually bargained for some proportion, an eighth, a tenth, or a thirteenth, of the produce. On the Mendips the lord of the soil received the tenth part as 'lot'; on the royal field of Derbyshire the king had the thirteenth, and at Alston the ninth dish of ore, the dish in the latter case being 'as much ore as a strong man can lift from the ground.' [148] At Alston the king had in addition the fifteenth penny from the other eight dishes, but had to provide at his own expense a man called 'the driver,' who understood how to separate the silver from the lead [149]. This method of paying a proportion of the produce was clearly the fairest to all concerned, for, as the Cumberland miners said in 1278, though they knew that there was ore enough to last to the end of time, no one could tell the yearly value of the mines, as it depended upon the richness of the ore they struck, [150] and in the same way when Robert de Thorp was made warden of the Devon mines in 1308, [151] it was expressly stated that no definite sum was to be demanded of him, because the silver-bearing ore, the refined lead, and the reworked slag all had 'diversetez de bonntez et quantitez de respouns.' In addition to the payment of lot ore, the miners had to give tithes to the Church. In some cases these tithes originated in a definite grant, more often they seem to have been regarded as compensation for the tithes of crops which would otherwise have grown on the ground taken by the mines; but the strangest reason for claiming them was that lead was itself a titheable crop, because it 'grew and renewed in the veins' [152]. While many small mines were worked by parties of free miners under these conditions, for their own profit, and at their own risk, there must have been from very early times a large number of poor men who worked for the king, the lord of the soil, or capitalist adventurers, receiving wages either by piece or by time. The regulations for the payment of these hired miners in the royal mines of Beer Alston, in Devonshire, drawn up in 1297 are of considerable interest [153].

'As to the piecework of the miners, those who can find ore in their diggings shall receive for piecework as before, that is to say 5s. for the load, [154] as well of black as of white ore, if the white cannot reasonably be put lower. And those who are engaged in "dead" (i.e., unremunerative) work, and cannot find ore in their diggings, and yet work more, for some dead work is harder than (digging in) the vein, shall be at wages (a lour soutz) until they reach the ore, so that all piecework be undertaken by two or three gangs who divide the profits between themselves, as well to those doing dead work as to the others.'

That the price of 5s. a load was calculated to pay the miners for their preliminary unproductive 'dead' work, may be gathered from the fact that 'tithe ore,' that is to say the ore paid to the Church, was bought back from the rector of Beer at 2s. the load, and a further 9d. was deducted from this sum for washing the ore [155]. At the same time it is clear that where the 'dead' work was exceptionally heavy or the eventual yield small this system of payment would not work; and in 1323 we find that the 'dead work' of clearing, searching, and digging into an old mine in Devon was paid at the rate of 3s. 4d. the fathom, and that two gangs of six men were paid at the daily rate of 7d.-9d., about 1½d. a head, for searching for the vein and for piercing the hard rock to follow up the vein in hope of finding a richer vein [156].

By the Ordinance of 1297 wages were to be paid every Saturday, though as a matter of fact we find that they were constantly falling into arrears.

'All the ore of each week shall be measured before the Saturday and carried to the boles or other places where it is to be smelted. And knowledge shall be taken each Saturday or Sunday of the issues of each week in all things. And the payments shall be made to the miners and other workmen the same Saturday. And no miner shall remain in a market town under colour of buying food, or in other manner after the ninth hour on Sunday, without leave.'

Besides their wages the miners received such iron, steel, and ropes as they required, free of charge, and had the use of a forge for the repair of their tools [157]. At Beer, in 1297, there were three forges, one for each of the three mines into which the field was divided, [158] and each worked by a man and a boy. In addition to the smiths [159] there would be, as auxiliaries, one or more candlemakers, carpenters, charcoal-burners, and woodcutters. In many mines it was also necessary to employ a number of hands in baling water out of the pits with leathern bodges or buckets; during April 1323 an average of twenty persons were so engaged at Beer Alston, and during one week the number rose to forty-eight [160]. So greatly did the accumulation of water in the pits interfere with work, that in early times the Devon mines were closed down during the winter, [161] and it was not until about 1297 that means were found of dealing with this evil. About that date the plan of draining the pits by means of 'avidods' or adits, that is to say horizontal galleries driven from the bottom of the pits to a level of free drainage on the surface, already in use in the tin mines, was introduced into the lead mines. The ordinances of 1297 arranged for one hundred tinners to work in 'avidods,' and the accounts of the working of these mines for the same year show payments averaging £12, 10s. to 'William Pepercorn and his partners,' and to six other gangs 'for making avidods' [162]. It was probably in the following year that Walter de Langton, Bishop of Chester, reported that the yield of the Beer mine had been doubled by the new method of draining, as they could now work as well in the winter as in the summer [163].

The ore having been raised was broken up with a hammer, no mechanical stamps being used apparently before the sixteenth century, if then, though there is mention in 1302 of a machine (ingenium) for breaking 'black work' or slag [164]. It was then washed in 'buddles' or troughs, with the aid of coarse sieves, women being frequently employed for this process. The washed ore, separated as far as possible from stone and other impurities, was then carried to the smelting furnace. The commonest type of furnace was the 'bole,' a rough stone structure like a limekiln, with an opening at the top, serving as a chimney, and also for charging the furnace, and one or more vents at the base for the blast. These boles were usually built in exposed and draughty positions, and could only be used when the wind was favourable. At an early date they were supplemented by 'slag-hearths' or furnaces (fornelli) possessing an artificial blast and closely resembling blacksmiths' forges. The bellows of these hearths were usually driven by the feet of men or women, but a water mill was in use in Devon at least as early as 1295, [165] and at Wolsingham, in Durham, in 1426 water power was used when available, the footblast being used during dry seasons [166]. The fuel of the boles was brushwood, and that of the hearths charcoal, with peat and, for the remelting of the lead, sea-coal. In Devon mention is made of a third type of smelting house, the 'hutte,' the nature of which is obscure. The huttes are usually classed with the boles; [167] thus it was noted in 1297 that 'from each load of black ore smelted at the huttes and boles there come 3½ feet of silver-lead, each foot containing 70 lbs. of lead, each pound weighing 25s. sterling. And from a load of black ore smelted by the mill furnace come 3 feet of silver-lead. And from a load of white ore smelted by the furnace or elsewhere come 1½ feet of silver-lead. Moreover a pound of lead made from black ore smelted by the boles and huttes and by their furnaces yields 2 dwt. of silver; a pound of lead from black ore smelted by the mill furnace yields 3 dwt. of silver; and a pound made from white ore 1½ dwt. 'In the same way the 'black work' or slag of both boles and huttes were reworked at the furnaces [168]. A possible hint is found in the fact that large quantities of refined lead had to be put into the hutte when it was first lit,'as the huttes cannot burn ore or smelt lead without the addition of sufficient melted lead at the start to roast (coquenda) the ore in the lead so added' [169]. This certainly suggests some sort of cupellation furnaces. Yet another type of furnace was the 'turn-hearth' used in the Mendips; the construction of this, again, is obscure, but it seems to have derived its name from some portion of the hearth being movable and adjustable to changing winds, while it would seem that the ordinary furnace could only be used when the wind blew from a particular quarter. [170] There are references in 1302 to a 'fornellus versatilis' used in the Devon mines, and one entry speaks of making the furnace 'upon the turning machine' (super ingenium versatile) [171].

The bolers and furnacemen, who were paid about 12d. to 16d. a week, their assistants receiving about half those amounts, having cast the lead into pigs and stamped it, handed it over to the wardens of the mine. The next process was the refining of the silver from the lead by cupellation. When an alloy of silver and lead is melted on an open hearth with free access of air, the lead is oxidized and, in the form of litharge, can be removed either by skimming it off or by absorption by the porous body of the hearth, leaving the silver in a more or less pure form. By adding more lead and repeating the process the silver can be further refined. In England it seems to have been usual to remove the litharge by absorption; in the case of the Romano-British refinery at Silchester, [172] the absorbent material used was bone ash, but in the medieval refineries at the Devon mines charred 'tan turves,' [173] or refuse blocks of oak bark from the tanneries, were used, and probably the same material was used in Derbyshire, the southern mines being largely worked by Derbyshire miners. A thick bed of this tan-ash was made with a dished hollow in the middle, in which was placed the fuel and the lead; the hearth was then fired and blast supplied from the side: when the whole was melted the fire was raked aside and the blast turned on to the upper surface of the molten metal, which was thus rapidly oxidized and so refined.

But first, as soon as the mass of silver-lead was in a fluid state, 'before the ash has absorbed any of the lead, the lead is to be stirred and mixed so that it is of equal quality throughout, and a quantity of the lead amounting to about 6s. weight shall be taken out, and this shall be divided into two parts, half being given to the refiner, ticketed with his name, and the date and sealed by the wardens, and the other half shall be assayed by the king's assayer in the presence of the wardens and of the refiner, and the refiner shall answer for the whole of that refining at the rate of the assay, as nearly as is reasonable, having regard to the fact that there is greater waste and loss in the big operation of refining than in the assay. And when the silver has been fully refined it shall be given by the refiners to the wardens for a tally (or receipt) of the weight, so that there shall be neither suspicion nor deceit on either side.... And the lead that remains in the ash after the refining shall be resmelted at a suitable time' [174]. These ordinances of 1297, just quoted, arranged for there being five skilled refiners at the Devon mines, and the account rolls show that they received from 18d. to 2s. a week.

The silver seems to have been cast into plates or ingots varying from ten to twenty pounds in weight and value (for the monetary pound was simply the pound weight of standard silver). Its purity probably varied, for while in 1296 the pound of refined silver was mixed with 14d. of alloy to bring it to the standard, [175] a few years later silver weighing £132, 5s. was worth only £131, 13s.

7¼d. in coined money, [176] and 370 lbs. of silver sent up from Martinstowe in 1294 had to be further refined in London before it could be made into silver vessels for the Countess of Barre. [177] In the case of the lead we have the usual medieval complexity of weights. An early entry [178] records that 'a carretate (or cartload) of lead of the Peak contains 24 fotinels, each of 70 lbs., and the fotinel contains 14 cuts [179] of 5 lbs. A carretate of London is larger by 420 lbs. ' The London weight appears to have gained the day, as a later entry gives 13½ lbs. to a stone, 6 stones to a foot, and 30 feet (or 2430 lbs.) to a carretate 'according to the weight of the Peak.' [180] In Devon we find in 1297 carretates of 24 feet and 32 feet in use simultaneously, the foot being 70 lbs. here as in Derbyshire [181].

In no other part of England had the lead-mining industry so continuous a history of steady prosperity as in Derbyshire. The Devon mines seem to have been richer and more productive during a short period, but the half century, 1290-1340 practically covers the period of their boom. During the five years, 1292-1297, these mines produced £4046 of silver, and about £360 worth of lead; next year the silver amounted to £1450. Then in April 1299 the king leased the mines to the Friscobaldi, Italian merchants and money-lenders, with whom he had many dealings [182]. They agreed to pay 13s. 4d. a load for the ore, but after about a year, during which time they drew some 3600 loads of ore, [183] they found that they were losing heavily, the ore not being worth more than 10s. a load, and the costs of working being higher than they had expected [184]. The mines, however, continued to yield well when worked by the king for his own benefit, as much as £1773 of silver and £180 from lead being obtained in 1305: this, however, seems to have been the highwater mark, the yield for 1347 being only £70 [185]. After this the mines were let to private adventurers from time to time; but such records as we have do not suggest that many fortunes were made from them: in 1426 the yield for the previous two and a half years had been 39 ounces of silver, [186] for the year 1442 it was £17, [187] but for the six years, 1445-51, the average output rose to 4000 ounces. [188] At the beginning of the boom, in 1295, it was found necessary to recruit labour from the older lead-mining districts, and commissioners were appointed to select miners for Devon from Cheshire, Earl Warenne's liberty of Bromfield in Shropshire, the Peak, Gloucester, Somerset, and Dorset [189]. The ordinances of 1297 stipulated for 150 miners from the Peak, and an equal number of local men from Devon and Cornwall, though the accounts show that there were that year 384 miners from the Peak, and 35 from Wales [190]. On the other hand, in 1296, while we have over 300 miners coming from the Peak, a twelve days' journey, we also find four picked men sent from Devon to the king's court, and thence to Ireland to prospect on the king's behalf [191].

The prosperity of the Devon mines caused an increase of activity in those of Somerset, where a number of fresh strikes were reported during the early years of the fourteenth century, about one of which an optimistic lead reeve wrote to the Bishop of Bath and Wells as follows: [192] — 'Know, my lord, that your workmen have found a splendid mine [193] of lead on the Mendips to the east of Priddy, and one that can be opened up with no trouble, being only five or six feet below the ground. And since these workmen are so often thieves, craftily separating the silver from the lead, stealthily taking it away, and when they have collected a quantity fleeing like thieves and deserting their work, as has frequently happened in times past, therefore your bailiffs are causing the ore to be carried to your court of Wookey where there is a furnace built at which the workmen smelt the ore under supervision of certain persons appointed by your steward. And as the steward, bailiffs, and workmen consider that there is a great deal of silver in the lead, on account of its whiteness and sonority, they beg that you will send them as soon as possible a good and faithful workman upon whom they can rely. I have seen the first piece of lead smelted there, of great size and weight, which when it is struck rings almost like silver, wherefore I agree with the others that if it is faithfully worked the business should prove of immense value to yourself and to the neighbourhood, and if a reliable workman is obtained I think that it would be expedient to smelt the ore where it is dug, on account of the labour of carrying so heavy material such a distance. The ore is in grains like sand.'

There is no evidence that this mine fulfilled the sanguine expectations of its discoverers, but about the same time, in 1314, we find Herman de Alemannia and other adventurers working a mine in Brushford, near Dulverton [194]. The Germans were for many centuries the most skilled miners, and English mining owes much to their enterprise. As an instance of their greater skill we may take the case of Thomas de Alemaigne, silver finer, [195] who being out of work petitioned the king to grant him the refuse and slag (les aftirwas et les remisailles) thrown aside at the mines in Devonshire, which had been refined so far as those at the mines could refine them: no one else would touch them, so the king would get no gain unless he granted them to Thomas, who was willing to pay 20s. a year for the right to rework them. This same Thomas de Alemaigne was appointed in 1324 to dig, cleanse, and examine the king's mines in Cumberland and Westmoreland [196]. Probably these mines had not been worked for some time previous, as in 1292 the total issues of the Alston mines for the last fourteen years were said to have been £4, 0s. 2d., possibly owing to the absence of fuel, which is given as the reason for an iron mine there being worth only 15s. a year [197]. Later, in 1359, Tilman de Cologne was farming the Alston mines, and in 1475, as a result apparently of a report by George Willarby [198] that there were in the north of England three notable mines, one containing 27 lbs. of silver to the fodder of lead with a vein half a rod broad, another 18 lbs. with a vein five rods broad, and the third 4 lbs. with a vein 1¼ rods broad, the mines of Blaunchlond in Northumberland, Fletchers in Alston, Keswick in Cumberland, and also the copper mine near Richmond, were granted for fifteen years to the Duke of Gloucester, the Earl of Northumberland, William Goderswyk, and John Marchall [199]. The two noblemen were presumably sleeping partners, and appear to have abandoned the arrangement, as soon afterwards, in 1478, William Goderswyk, Henry Van Orel, Arnold van Anne, and Albert Millyng of Cologne, and Dederic van Riswyk of England, received a grant for ten years of all mines of gold, silver, copper, and lead in Northumberland, Cumberland, and Westmoreland, paying one- fifteenth of the profits [200].

Although gold is mentioned in this last entry and in a number of other grants of mines in the fifteenth century, and though Galias de Lune and his partners were licensed in 1462 to dig ores containing gold in Gloucestershire and Somerset, [201] gold does not appear to have been worked in paying quantities in England. In 1325 John de Wylwringword was sent down to the mines of Devon and Cornwall to seek for gold: he obtained from the Devon mines 22 dwt., of which he refined 3 dwt. at Exeter; this yielded 2½ dwt. of pure gold [202]. The remainder was sent up to the Exchequer and eventually refined at York; but this is almost the only note we have of gold being found, though no doubt small quantities were found from time to time in the Cornish stream tinworks.

In 1545 one St. Clere declared that certain gold called 'gold hoppes and gold oore' in every stream tinwork in Devon and Cornwall was by ignorance of the tinners molten with the tin, and so conveyed abroad; certain persons were appointed to test his statement [203].

Chapter 4

MINING—TIN

Tin mining claims an antiquity unsurpassed by any other industry in this country, but with what degree of justice may well be doubted. The claim of the western promontory of Britain, later known as Cornwall and Devon, to be the Cassiterides or Tin Islands whence the Phœnicians obtained their stores of that metal at least five hundred years before the Christian era rests upon rather shadowy grounds [204]. Diodorus Siculus, who wrote about B.C. 30, is the first writer definitely to connect Britain with the tin trade, and his statements appear to be based rather upon a doubtful understanding of earlier topographers than upon actual knowledge. According to him the tin was produced in the promontory of 'Bolerium' and brought to the island of 'Ictis,' whence it was transported to Gaul. If 'Bolerium' is Cornwall, then there is no reason to doubt that 'Ictis' is 'Insula Vectis,' or the Isle of Wight, which was at that date still connected to the mainland by a narrow ridge of rock, covered at highwater, but dry at low water, as 'Ictis' is said to have been [205]. It is certainly strange, if an ancient and well-established trade in tin really existed in Britain when the Romans came over, that that race, with its keen eye for metallic wealth, should have made no use of the tin mines of Cornwall. Yet there is no reference to these mines in the literature of the period of the Roman occupation, nor are there traces of anything approaching an occupation of Cornwall by the Romans, who appear to have ignored this corner of Britain completely. After the departure of the Romans, and before the Saxons conquered this district, which did not happen till the middle of the tenth century, there is some evidence of tin being worked here, as Cornish tin is said to have been carried over to France in the seventh century, and in a life of St. John of Alexandria, who died in 616, there is a story of an Alexandrian galley coming to Britain for tin [206]. That the Saxons worked the tin seems probable from the discovery of Saxon remains in the St. Austell tin grounds and elsewhere, [207] but the industry can hardly have been of any great importance at the time of the Norman Conquest, as there is no reference to it in the Domesday Survey.

While the history of tin mining in Britain prior to the middle of the twelfth century is problematical, there is from that time onwards an immense mass of material bearing upon the subject. This material has been patiently examined by Mr. George Randall Lewis, and summarised in his work on The Stannaries, [208] a book so full and complete that I have saved myself much labour by basing this chapter almost entirely upon it.

There are, as might be expected, many analogies between the mining of tin and the mining of lead. The processes were very similar, and the laws governing the workers had much in common, but it is in the case of the Stannaries that we find the full development of the 'free miner,' so far as England is concerned. Certain initial differences in the methods employed are observable owing to the form in which tin is obtained. Tin, like other metals, exists in veins or lodes embedded in the rock at various depths; where these veins outcrop on the banks of a stream they are broken up by the action of the water and climatic variations, the resultant pile of stanniferous boulders being known as 'shode'; the waters of the stream constantly wear away small pieces of the tin ore and carry it downwards until, owing to its heavy specific gravity, the tin sinks, forming a deposit in the bed of the stream which may sometimes be as much as twenty feet thick. It was this third class of alluvial tin which was alone worked in prehistoric and early medieval days. This might safely be assumed, but rather remarkable confirmation is obtained from an account of tin worked for Edmund of Cornwall in 1297. From this it appears that twenty-eight and a half 'foot-fates' of ore produced a thousand-weight (1200 lbs.) of 'white tin,' the proportion corresponding pretty closely with those—three 'foot-fates' of ore to yield 105 lbs. of metal—given in the sixteenth century by Thomas Beare for alluvial or 'stream' tin, which was far richer than mine tin [209]. It cannot have been very long before the miners realised that the stream tin was carried down by the water, and shadowy grounds [204]. Diodorus Siculus, who wrote about B.C. 30, is the first writer definitely to connect Britain with the tin trade, and his statements appear to be based rather upon a doubtful understanding of earlier topographers than upon actual knowledge. According to him the tin was produced in the promontory of 'Bolerium' and brought to the island of 'Ictis,' whence it was transported to Gaul. If

'Bolerium' is Cornwall, then there is no reason to doubt that 'Ictis' is 'Insula Vectis,' or the Isle of Wight, which was at that date still connected to the mainland by a narrow ridge of rock, covered at highwater, but dry at low water, as 'Ictis' is said to have been [205]. It is certainly strange, if an ancient and well-established trade in tin really existed in Britain when the Romans came over, that that race, with its keen eye for metallic wealth, should have made no use of the tin mines of Cornwall. Yet there is no reference to these mines in the literature of the period of the Roman occupation, nor are there traces of anything approaching an occupation of Cornwall by the Romans, who appear to have ignored this corner of Britain completely. After the departure of the Romans, and before the Saxons conquered this district, which did not happen till the middle of the tenth century, there is some evidence of tin being worked here, as Cornish tin is said to have been carried over to France in the seventh century, and in a life of St. John of Alexandria, who died in 616, there is a story of an Alexandrian galley coming to Britain for tin [206]. That the Saxons worked the tin seems probable from the discovery of Saxon remains in the St. Austell tin grounds and elsewhere, [207] but the industry can hardly have been of any great importance at the time of the Norman Conquest, as there is no reference to it in the Domesday Survey.

While the history of tin mining in Britain prior to the middle of the twelfth century is problematical, there is from that time onwards an immense mass of material bearing upon the subject. This material has been patiently examined by Mr. George Randall Lewis, and summarised in his work on The Stannaries, [208] a book so full and complete that I have saved myself much labour by basing this chapter almost entirely upon it.

There are, as might be expected, many analogies between the mining of tin and the mining of lead. The processes were very similar, and the laws governing the workers had much in common, but it is in the case of the Stannaries that we find the full development of the 'free miner,' so far as England is concerned. Certain initial differences in the methods employed are observable owing to the form in which tin is obtained. Tin, like other metals, exists in veins or lodes embedded in the rock at various depths; where these veins outcrop on the banks of a stream they are broken up by the action of the water and climatic variations, the resultant pile of stanniferous boulders being known as 'shode'; the waters of the stream constantly wear away small pieces of the tin ore and carry it downwards until, owing to its heavy specific gravity, the tin sinks, forming a deposit in the bed of the stream which may sometimes be as much as twenty feet thick. It was this third class of alluvial tin which was alone worked in prehistoric and early medieval days. This might safely be assumed, but rather remarkable confirmation is obtained from an account of tin worked for Edmund of Cornwall in 1297. From this it appears that twenty-eight and a half 'foot-fates' of ore produced a thousand-weight (1200 lbs.) of 'white tin,' the proportion corresponding pretty closely with those—three 'foot-fates' of ore to yield 105 lbs. of metal—given in the sixteenth century by Thomas Beare for alluvial or 'stream' tin, which was far richer than mine tin [209]. It cannot have been very long before the miners realised that the stream tin was carried down by the water, and started to search for its source. The 'shode,' or boulder tin, must therefore have been worked almost as early as the alluvial deposits, and the final stage was the working of the 'lode.' In this lode mining the first workings were no doubt shallow trenches and confined to places where the ore lay close to the surface; a somewhat greater depth was obtained by 'shamelling,' the trench being carried down in stages, a 'shamell' or platform being left at each stage at the height to which the miner could throw his ore; finally came the deep shaft with galleries. But here, as in all mining, the question of drainage came in. Where the workings were quite shallow the water could be baled out with wooden bowls, or a 'level,' or deep ditch, could be dug. For greater depths the adit, or drainage gallery (see above, p. 50), was available, and although Mr. Lewis [210] cannot find any instance of the use of the adit in tin mining before the seventeenth century, it does not seem reasonable to doubt that it was in use much earlier. Exactly when pumps and other draining machines were introduced into the tin mines is not clear, but probably they were little used during our medieval period, when few of the mines were of any great depth [211].

The primitive miner, when he had got his ore with the aid of his simple tools, a wooden shovel and a pick, also in earliest times of wood, but later of iron, constructed a rough hearth of stones on which he kindled a fire. When it was burning strongly he cast in his ore and afterwards collected the molten tin from the ashes. The next stage was to construct a regular furnace, exactly similar in type to the boles or furnaces used for lead-melting (see above, p. 51). These furnaces were enclosed in a building, the 'blowing-house,' in early times a rough thatched shanty, which was burnt from time to time to obtain the metallic dust which had lodged in the thatch, but afterwards more substantial. The cost of a 'melting howse' (80 feet by 20 feet) built at Larian in Cornwall by Burcord Crangs, a German, in the time of Queen Mary, was about £300, composed as follows: [212] —

For the ryddyng, clensing and leveling of the ground for setting of the foundacon therof

£23
6
8

For making foundacon of the walls and the poynyons of the meltyng howse

120
0
0

For making of the audit [213] to build the fornas and meltyng chymney upon

30
0
0

For tymbering and covering the howse with esclattes

50
0
0

For dores, windows, locks, and barres

6
0
0

The whele, exultree and the stampers

10
0
0

For 4 paire of grete bellowes wt their geames and other necessaryes

20
0
0

For makyng of the Colehouse

15
0
0

For makyng of the Rostingehowse [214]

20
0
0

For makyng of the lete and dyke comyng to the meltynghowse

66
0
0

For the hatt and the crane

20
0
0

The lumps of ore were first broken up with hammers or in a mill; the powdered ore was then washed to free it as far as possible from earthy impurities. Sometimes this was done with a 'vanne,' or shovel, the heavy ore remaining at the point of the shovel and the lighter impurities being washed away. An elaborate process was also used, in which the water containing the powdered ore was allowed to run over pieces of turf, the metallic portion sinking and becoming entangled in the fibres. The usual method, however, was by means of troughs or 'buddles.' This washing was not only a necessary preliminary to the smelting, but had an economic importance, as it was at the wash that the ore was divided when a claim was worked by partners, and the tribute or share due to the lord of the soil was apportioned; it was also, towards the end of the medieval period, the only place where the ore might be bought by dealers [215]. To prevent fraud it was therefore enacted that due notice should be given of washes, and no secret buddles should be used.

When we first get any details of tin-working, in 1198, it was usual for the tin to be smelted twice, the first being a rough process performed near the tinfield, but the second, or refining, being only permitted at special places and in the presence of the officers of the stannaries. The tin from the first smelting had to be stamped by the royal officers within two weeks of smelting, a toll being paid to the king at the same time of 2s. 6d. per thousand-weight in Devon, and of 5s. in Cornwall. Moreover, by the regulations of 1198, within thirteen weeks the tin had to be resmelted and again stamped, this time paying a tax of one mark [216]. The double smelting possibly ceased before the end of the thirteenth century. In any case the fiscal arrangement was altered, and in 1302, not long after the stannaries had reverted to the Crown, after being in the hands of the Earls of Cornwall from 1231 to 1300, we find the stampage dues consolidated into a single coinage duty. Under this system of coinage all the tin smelted had to be sent to certain specified towns, those for Cornwall being Bodmin, Liskeard, Lostwithiel, Helston, and Truro; and for Devon, Chagford, Tavistock, Plympton, and Ashburton. Here the tin remained until the two yearly visits of the coinage officials, at Michaelmas and Midsummer, when each block, weighing roughly 200 to 300 lbs., was assayed, weighed, and taxed: it was then stamped and might be sold. To prevent fraud an elaborate system of marking was gradually introduced during the sixteenth and seventeenth centuries, and the use of private marks by the owners of the blowing-houses was probably of much earlier origin. The use of these marks was designed not only to protect the merchant, but also to act as a check on smuggling, of which an immense amount undoubtedly went on [217].

One result of the coinage system, by which tin might not be sold until stamped, and could only be stamped twice a year, was that the smaller tin-workers inevitably fell into the hands of the capitalists. The small independent tinner, with no reserve of capital to draw upon, had almost always to pledge his tin in advance to the adventurers and tin-dealers, and as a result he was often worse off with his theoretical independence than he would have been as a recognised wage- labourer. The wage work system must have been introduced into the stannaries at quite an early period. Even in 1237 there are references to servants who worked the mines for the tinners [218]. In 1342 certain of the wealthier Cornish tinners endeavoured to force their poorer brethren to work for them at a penny a day, when they had been working tin worth 20d. or more daily, and it is said that Abraham the tinner in 1357 was actually employing three hundred persons on his works. Side by side with these hired workmen were the independent tinners, working either separately or, more usually in partnerships; but from the small amounts which many of these tinners presented for coinage, Mr. Lewis has concluded that they may have been only partly dependent upon their mining [219]. There is, however, the complication that the small amounts presented may in part have been due to their having sold their ore to the larger dealers, but it is clear that some of the tinners did also carry on farming.

While the economic position of the smaller tinners must often have been little, if at all, superior to that of ordinary labourers, their political position was remarkable. They constituted a state within a state; the free miner 'paid taxes not as an Englishman, but as a miner. His law was not the law of the realm, but that of his mine. He obeyed the king only when his orders were communicated through the warden of the mines, and even then so long only as he respected the mining law. His courts were the mine courts, his parliament the mine parliament' [220]. The tinner was a free man and could not be subjected to the system of villeinage. He had the right of prospecting anywhere within the two counties, except in churchyards, highways, and gardens, and might 'bound' or stake out a claim by the simple process of cutting shallow holes and making piles of turf at the four corners of his claim, and such claim would be his absolute property provided that he worked it (the exact amount of work necessary to retain a claim varied in different places and at different periods). For his claim he paid to the lord of the land, whether it were the king or a private lord, a certain tribute of ore, usually the tenth or the fifteenth portion. He had, moreover, the right to divert streams, either to obtain water for washing his ore, or to enable him to dig in the bed of the stream, and the important privilege of compelling landowners to sell him fuel for his furnace. Further, he had his own courts, and was under the sole jurisdiction of the warden-officers of the stannaries. Each stannary, of which there were five in Cornwall and four in Devon, had its own court, presided over by a steward, and no tinner might plead or be impleaded outside his court, from which the appeal lay to the warden, or in practice to the vice-warden. How and when these privileges were obtained must remain a matter for speculation, but they can be traced when William de Wrotham was appointed warden in 1198, and were definitely confirmed to the tinners by King John in 1201. By development, apparently, from the two yearly great courts of the stannaries, arose the 'stannary parliaments.' The parliament for Cornwall consisted of twenty-four members, six being nominated by the mayor and council of each of the four towns of Lostwithiel, Launceston, Truro, and Helston; that of Devon contained ninety-six members, twenty-four from each of the stannaries. Those parliaments were summoned, through the lord warden, by the Duke of Cornwall, in whom the supreme control of the stannaries was vested from 1338 onwards, and had power not only to legislate for the stannaries, but to veto any national legislation which infringed their privileges. When the parliaments originated is not known, but they were certainly established before the beginning of the sixteenth century, prior to which date all records of their proceedings are lost.

With all these privileges, to which may be added exemption from ordinary taxation and military service, though the tinners were liable to be taxed separately and enrolled for service under their own officers, it was natural that the exact definition of a tinner should have given rise to much dispute. On the one hand, it was argued that these exemptions and privileges applied only to working tinners actually employed in getting ore; on the other, the tin dealers, blowers, and owners of blowing-houses claimed to be included. Eventually the larger definition was accepted, and, indeed, it was almost entirely from the capitalist section of the industry that the parliaments were elected, from the sixteenth century, if not earlier.

It is rather remarkable that when the stannaries first come into evidence, in the reign of Henry II. , the chief centre of production appears to have been Devon rather than Cornwall [221]. So far as can be estimated the output during this reign rose gradually from about 70 tons in 1156 to about 350 in 1171. Richard I., with his constant need of money, reorganised the stannaries in 1198, and at the beginning of John's reign the output was between 400 and 450 tons. The issue of the charter to the stannaries in 1201 does not seem to have had any immediate effect on the industry, but about ten years later there was increased activity, the output rising in 1214 to 600 tons [222]. During the early years of Henry III. the tin revenues were farmed out, and no details are available either for these years, or from the period 1225-1300, during which time the stannaries were in the hands of the Earls of Cornwall. Two things only are clear, that the total output had fallen off, and that Cornwall had now far outstripped Devon. The grant of a charter confirming the privileges of the stannaries in 1305 seems to have marked the beginning of a more prosperous era, and by 1337 the output had reached 700 tons. The Black Death, however, in 1350 put an end to this prosperity, and with the exception of a boom during the reign of Henry IV. tinning did not recover until just at the end of our medieval period. Even at its worst, however, the industry was a source of considerable revenue, the coinage duties [223] never falling below £1000, and amounting in 1337 and 1400 to over £3000, in addition to which there were other smaller payments and perquisites [224]. The royal privileges of pre-emption was also of value to needy kings who frequently availed themselves of it to grant this pre-emption, or virtual monopoly, to wealthy foreign merchants and other money-lenders in return for substantial loans.

Before leaving the subject of the tin mines of Cornwall and Devon, it is perhaps worth while noting that there is virtually no documentary evidence of the working of the copper deposits of Cornwall prior to the late sixteenth century, and it would seem that most of the copper used in medieval England must have been imported.

Chapter 5

QUARRYING—STONE, MARBLE, ALABASTER, CHALK

Stone-quarrying is an industry to which the references in medieval records are more numerous than enlightening. It would be easy to fill pages with a list of casual references to the working of quarries in all parts of England, and after struggling through the list the reader would know that stone was dug in quite a lot of places at different times, which he might have assumed without the documentary evidence. It is natural that when a castle, an abbey, a church, or other stone building is to be erected the stone, whose cost lies mainly in transport, should be obtained from the nearest possible source. Founders of monasteries frequently made grants either of existing quarries or of the right to dig stone for the monastic buildings, and the discovery of a bed of suitable stone close to the site selected for the Conqueror's votive abbey of Battle was so opportune as to be deemed a miracle [225]. When a monastery was founded in a district where stone could not be found, it was almost essential that its supplies should be drawn if possible from some place from which the stone could be carried by water, and it was no doubt the position of Barnack between the Welland and the Nene that made its quarries so important to the monks of the Fenland [226]. The abbeys of Peterborough, Ramsey, Crowland, Bury St. Edmund and Sawtry all held quarries in Barnack and quarrelled amongst themselves over their respective rights. The monks of Sawtry, for instance, had made a canal for carrying stone to their abbey by way of Wittlesea Mere by permission of the abbey of Ramsey, a permission which they seem to have abused, as in 1192 orders were given to block all their lodes except the main one leading to Sawtry, and they had to promise to put up no buildings except one rest house for the men on their stone barges [227].

For York Minster [228] stone was brought from the quarries of Thevesdale, Huddleston, and Tadcaster down the Wharfe, and from Stapleton down the Aire into the Ouse, and so up to St. Leonard's wharf, whence it was carried on sleds to the mason's yard. Westminster and London were mainly supplied from Surrey, from the Reigate and Chaldon quarries, and Kent, from the Maidstone district. The tough 'Kentish rag,' which was used by the Romans for the walls of London, was much in demand for the rougher masonry, [229] and in a contract for building a wharf by the Tower in 1389, it was stipulated that the core of the walls should be of 'raggs,' and the facing of 'assheler de Kent' [230]. The Reigate stone, on the other hand, was of superior quality and more suited for fine work, and we find it constantly used for images, carved niches, and window tracery [231].

The most accessible stone not always being the most suitable for the varying requirements of architecture, it was necessary to find other stone possessing the desired qualities, and certain quarries at an early date acquired renown. Setting aside the famous Norman quarries of Caen, whose stone appears in greater or less quantities in hundreds of buildings and of records, there are a number of English quarries of more than local repute in medieval times. Such were the quarries of Beer in Devonshire, from whose labyrinthine galleries stone was carried to Rochester in 1367, [232] to St. Stephen's Westminster in 1362, [233] and elsewhere. The fine limestone, later known as Bath Stone, was quarried to a large extent at Haslebury in Box in Wiltshire, from which place it was sent in 1221 to the royal palace at Winchester for the columns of the hall and for chimney hoods, [234] Richard Sired receiving 23s. 4d. for cutting 105 blocks of stone in the quarry of Hesalburi [235]. For these same works at Winchester much stone was brought from the Hampshire quarry of Selebourne, and from the better known quarries of the Isle of Wight, while a stone-cutter was sent to procure material from the quarry of Corfe. This latter was no doubt the same as the 'hard stone of Corfe,' bought for Westminster in 1278 [236]. With Corfe and Purbeck is associated Portland stone, which attained its greatest fame in the hands of Wren after the Fire of London, but was already appreciated in the fourteenth century, when it was used in Exeter Cathedral and at Westminster [237]. Further east Sussex possessed a number of quarries of local importance, [238] and the quarry of green sandstone at Eastbourne, from which the great Roman walls of Pevensey and the medieval castle within them were alike built, probably provided the '28 stones of Burne, worked for windows of the vault under the chapel' at Shene in 1441 [239]. Another Sussex quarry, that of Fairlight, near Hastings, supplied large quantities of stone for Rochester Castle in 1366 and 1367 [240].

The list of stone brought in the latter year at Rochester is of interest as showing the various sources from which it was derived [241]. There were bought 55 tons of Beer freestone at prices varying from 9s. to 10s. the ton, [242] 62 tons of Caen stone at 9s., 45 tons of Stapleton freestone [243] at 8s., 44 tons of Reigate stone at 6s., 195 tons of freestone from Fairlight at 3s. 4d., 1850 tons of rag from Maidstone at 40s. the hundred tons, and a large quantity [244] of worked stone from Boughton Mounchelsea.

The Kentish quarries seem to have been especially favoured for the manufacture of the stone balls flung by the royal artillery, in early days by mangonels, balistae, and other forms of catapults, and in later days by guns. Thus in 1342 the sheriff of Kent accounted for £13, 10s. spent on 300 stones dug in the quarry of Folkestone and drawn out of the sea in various places, and afterwards cut and hewn into round balls for the king's machines; one hundred weighing 600 lbs. each, and the same number 500 lbs. and 400 lbs. respectively; and a further £7, 10s. for another 300 stone balls of various weights [245]. It is true that some years earlier, in 1333, similar balls had been obtained in Yorkshire, the sheriff buying 19 damlades [246] and 3 tons of stone in the quarry of Tadcaster, and setting 37 masons to work, the result being 606 stone balls weighing 9 damlades, [247] but casual references point to Kent as the great centre of manufacture. In 1418 as many as 7000 such balls were ordered to be made at Maidstone and elsewhere, and the Maidstone quarries were still turning out stone shot for bombards during the early years of Henry VIII. [248].

So far we have been dealing with what may be called block stone, but there were also in many parts of the country stones that from the ease with which they could be split into thin slabs were suitable for roofing purposes. How early, and to what extent the true slates of Cornwall and Devon were worked it is difficult to say, but in 1296, when certain buildings were put up for the miners at Martinestowe 23,000 'sclattes' were quarried at Birlond, and another 10,000 at 'Hassal' [249]. For the roofing of buildings at Restormel in Cornwall in 1343 slates were employed, 19,500 being bought 'between Golant and Fowey,' at 11d. the thousand, and 85,500 dug in the quarry of Bodmatgan at a cost of 6d. the thousand [250]. So also in 1385, at Lostwithiel, it is probable that the 'tiles,' of which 25,400 were bought 'in the quarry' at 3s. 4d. the thousand were true slates [251]. But besides the real slates, which in their modern uniformity of perfection render so many towns hideous, there were many quarries of stone slates, of which the most famous were at Collyweston in Northants [252]. The Collyweston stone after being exposed to the influence of frost could easily be split into thin slabs, [253] and seem to have been used for roofing purposes as early as the times of the Romans. During the medieval period there are numerous references to these Collyweston slates, and about the end of the fourteenth century they seem to have fetched from 6s. to 8s. the thousand [254]. Other similar quarries of more than local fame were situated round Horsham in Sussex, [255] and Horsham slates continued in demand from early days until the diminished solidity of house construction made a less weighty, and incidentally less picturesque, material requisite for roofing.

The work of quarrying stone counted as unskilled labour, and the rate of pay of quarriers is almost always that of the ordinary labourer. At Martinstow in 1296, men 'breaking stone in the quarry' received 1½d. to 2d. a day, and women, always the cheapest form of labour, 1d. a day for carrying the stones from the quarry [256]. The Windsor accounts for 1368 show quarriers at Bisham (Bustesham) receiving 3½d. a day, and one, no doubt the foreman, 4d., while 65,000 blocks of stone were cut at 'Colingle' at 10s. the thousand, and 3500 at Stoneden at 20s [257]. Those employed upon shaping the rough blocks were naturally paid at a higher rate, and in 1333, while the quarriers at Tadcaster were paid 1s. 4d. a week, the masons employed there in making stone balls earned 2s. 6d., and their foremen 3s. a week [258]. Often, however, the payment was by piece work, and in the case of the stone wrought at Boughton Monchelsea in 1366 for Rochester Castle, we have a list of the rates of payment: 'rough ashlar' worked at 10s. the hundred, 'parpainassheler'—for mullions—cut to pattern 18s. the hundred, newel pieces 12d. each, jambs 3d. the foot, 'scu' or bevelled stones 2d. the foot, voussoirs (vausur) 5d. the foot, and so on [259]. The tools used were of a simple nature; the inventory of tools at Stapleton quarry in 1400 [260] shows a number of iron wedges, iron rods, 'gavelokes' or crowbars, iron hammers, 'pulyng axes,' [261] 'brocheaxes' and shovels.

So far we have been dealing with stone as a building material, but there were two varieties of stone worked in England in medieval times whose value was artistic rather than utilitarian. These were marble and alabaster. Purbeck Marble, [262] a dark shell conglomerate capable of receiving a very high polish, came into fashion towards the end of the twelfth century, and continued in great demand for some two hundred years. Not only was it used in 1205 at Chichester Cathedral, but it would seem that some thirty years earlier it was sent to Dublin and to Durham. All the evidence goes to show that the marble was not only quarried at Purbeck, but worked into columns and carved upon the spot, and it is probable that most, if not all, of the scores of marble effigies which still remain in churches, such as the figures of knights in the Temple Church and the tomb of King John at Worcester, were carved by members of the Purbeck school [263] and usually at the quarries, though in some cases it would seem that the carver was called upon to do his work at the place where it was to be used, and under the eye of his patron. But however much we may admire the execution of these Purbeck effigies, we must not hastily assume that they bear any particular resemblance to the persons whom they commemorate; for although the Purbeck carvers were no doubt capable of executing portrait sculpture, a large proportion of their work was undoubtedly conventional. Thus in 1253 we find Henry III. ordering the sheriff of Dorset to cause 'an image of a queen' to be cut in marble and carried to the nunnery of Tarrant Keynston, there to be placed over the tomb of his sister, the late Queen of Scots [264].

Corfe was the great centre of the Purbeck marble industry. William of Corfe who executed the tomb of 'Henry the King's son,' at Westminster in 1273, [265] was probably William le Blund, brother of Robert le Blund, also called Robert of Corfe, who supplied marble for the Eleanor crosses at Waltham, Northampton, and Lincoln; and one Adam of Corfe settled in London early in the fourteenth century, and died there in 1331. This Adam 'the marbler' seems to have carried out several large contracts, including the paving of St. Paul's, and in 1324 supplied great quantities of marble for the columns of St. Stephen's, Westminster, at 6d. the foot [266]. The same price was paid in 1333 for similar columns bought from Richard Canon, [267] one of a family which for a century and a half played a prominent part as carvers and marble merchants, particularly in connection with Exeter Cathedral.

By the sixteenth century, and probably for some time earlier, the 'Marblers and Stone Cutters of Purbeck' had formed themselves into a company. By their rules the industry was restricted to freemen of the company, and regulations were laid down as to the number of apprentices that might be employed. These apprentices, in turn, could become freemen at the end of seven years upon payment to the court held at Corfe Castle on Shrove Tuesday of 6s. 8d. and the render of a penny loaf and two pots of beer. The wives of freemen were also allowed to join the company on payment of 1s., and in that case might carry on the trade, with the assistance of an apprentice, after their husband's death. At the time, however, that this company was formed, it is probable that the greater part of their business was concerned with building stone, as the marble had gone out of fashion and been largely superseded by alabaster in the fifteenth century for sepulchral monuments.

Alabaster appears to have been dug in the neighbourhood of Tutbury in very early times, some of the Norman mouldings of the west door of Tutbury church being carved in this material [268]. It is in the same neighbourhood, at

Hanbury, that the earliest known sepulchral image in alabaster is to be found: this dates from the early years of the fourteenth century, but it was not until the middle of that century that the vogue of alabaster began. From 1360 onwards there exists a magnificent series of alabaster monuments which bear striking testimony to the skill of the medieval English carvers, [269] and it is clear from records and the evidence of such fragments as have survived the triple iconoclasm of Reformers, Puritans, and Churchwardens that these monuments found worthy companions in the statues and carved reredoses scattered throughout the churches of England [270]. One of the finest of these reredoses must have been the 'table of alabaster' bought in 1367 for the high altar of St. George's, Windsor. For this the enormous sum of £200 (more than £3000 of modern money) was paid to Peter Mason of Nottingham, while some idea of its size may be gathered from the fact that it took ten carts, each with eight horses, to bring it from Nottingham to Windsor, the journey occupying seventeen days [271].

All the evidence points to Nottingham having been the great centre of the industry, the material being brought from the Derbyshire quarries of Chellaston. The stone and the workmanship alike found favour outside this country, and in 1414, when the abbot of Fécamp required alabaster he sent his mason, Alexander de Berneval, to England to procure it; and it was from Thomas Prentis of Chellaston that the stone was bought [272]. The alabaster tomb of John, Duke of Bretagne, which was erected in Nantes Cathedral in 1408, was made in England by Thomas Colyn, Thomas Holewell, and Thomas Poppehowe, [273] but it is not certain that they belonged to Nottingham. Various customs accounts [274] show that carved alabaster figures were often exported to the Continent, and Mr. Hope has shown that a number of carvings still to be seen in the churches of France, and even of Iceland, [275] have the green background, with circular groups of red and white spots, peculiar to the Nottingham school [276].

Thomas Prentis, who is mentioned above, is found in 1419 in company with Robert Sutton [277] covenanting to carve, paint, and gild the elaborate and beautiful tomb of Ralph Green and his wife, which may still be seen in Lowick Church, Northants, for a sum of £40. An examination of this tomb makes it almost certain that the glorious monuments of the Earl and Countess of Arundel at Arundel, Henry IV. and Queen Joan at Canterbury, and the Earl of Westmoreland and his two wives at Staindrop, were all from the same workshop. During the last twenty years of the fifteenth and the first thirty years of the sixteenth century, we have the names of a number of 'alablastermen' and 'image-makers' in Nottingham, [278] Nicholas Hill in particular being prominent as a manufacturer of the popular St. John the Baptist heads, [279] and during the same period we find a number of 'alblasterers' at York [280]. At Burton-on-Trent, also, where Leland in the sixteenth century mentions 'many marbellers working in alabaster,' the trade was evidently established in 1481, when Robert Bocher and Gilbert Twist were working for a number of religious houses; and it still flourished there in 1581 and 1585, when Richard and Gabriel Royley undertook contracts for elaborate tombs of alabaster, [281] but for all practical purposes the English school of alabaster carvers ceased to exist when the Reformation put an end to the demand for images and carven tables.

The alabaster, or gypsum, when not suitable for carving, was still valuable for conversion into plaster by burning, the finer varieties yielding the so-called Plaster of Paris and the coarser the ordinary builders' plaster. References to the actual burning of plaster seem practically non- existent, but it is noteworthy that one of the places from which Plaster of Paris was obtained for the works at York Minster was Buttercrambe, [282] where there is a large deposit of gypsum which probably furnished the York alabasterers with their material. In the same way Chalk, though to some extent used for masonry, was most in demand for conversion into lime. When building operations of any importance were undertaken, it was usual to build a limekiln on the spot for the burning of the lime required for mortar. In earlier times the kiln seems to have taken the form of a pit, 'lymeputt' or, in Latin, puteus, being the term usually employed, but in 1400 we find a regular kiln (torale) built, 3300 bricks and 33 loads of clay being purchased for the purpose [283]. Where lime was burnt commercially, that is to say for sale and not merely for use on the spot, the kilns would naturally be larger and more permanent, and a sixteenth-century account of the erection of eight such kilns [284] at a place unnamed—probably Calais—shows that each kiln was 20 feet high, with walls 10 feet thick, and an average internal breadth of 10 feet, and cost over £450.

When wood was plentiful it was naturally employed for burning the lime, and a presentment made in 1255 with regard to the forest of Wellington mentions that the king's two limekilns (rees calcis) had devoured 500 oaks between them [285]. But it was soon found that pit coal was the best fuel for the purpose, and it was constantly used from the end of the thirteenth century onwards, as much as 1166 quarters of sea coal being bought in 1278 for the kilns (chauffornia) in connection with the work at the Tower [286]. For the most part, chalk and lime required for work at London or Westminster was brought from Greenwich. Kent has indeed always been one of the great centres of the trade, both home and foreign, and in 1527, [287] to take but one instance, we find six ships from Dutch ports taking out of Sandwich port chalk to the value of £20 [288]. In the chalk hills round Chislehurst labyrinthine galleries of great extent bear witness to the flourishing state of chalk-quarrying in this district in former times; [289] smaller quarries of a similar type exist in the 'caverns' at Guildford. Kent, Surrey, and Sussex [290] were indeed busily employed in quarrying chalk during the medieval period, and for long afterwards, down to the present day.

Chapter 6

METAL WORKING

The English craftsmen were renowned for their metal work from the days of St. Dunstan downwards. St. Dunstan was the patron of the goldsmiths, his image being one of the chief ornaments of their guild hall in London, and a ring attributed to his workmanship was in the possession of Edward I. in 1280, [291] while his tools, including the identical tongs with which he pulled the devil by the nose, may still be seen at Mayfield. Coming to later times and the less questionable evidence of records, we may probably see in Otto the Goldsmith, whose name occurs in the Domesday Survey of 1086, the progenitor of the family of Fitz-Otho, king's goldsmiths and masters of the Mint from 1100 to 1300 [292]. The names of many early goldsmiths [293] have survived, and the beautiful candlestick given to St. Peter's Abbey at Gloucester in 1110, and now in the South Kensington Museum, is evidence of their mastery of the art. The great religious houses were foremost patrons of the craft, many of them, as the Abbey of St. Albans, numbering amongst their inmates artists of great repute. The famous college of Beverley included a goldsmith in its household, [294] but in 1292, when it was determined to erect a new shrine for the relics of St. John of Beverley, the chapter did not entrust the work to their own craftsman, but sent up to London to the establishment of William Faringdon, the greatest goldsmith of that time. The contract between his servant, Roger of Faringdon, and the Chapter of Beverley is still extant [295]. By it the chapter were to provide the necessary silver and gold; Roger was to refine it, if needful, and to supply his own coals, quicksilver, and other materials. The shrine was to be 5 ft. 6 in. long, 1 ft. 6 in. broad, and of proportionate height: the design was to be architectural in style, and the statuettes, the number and size of which were to be at the discretion of the chapter, were to be of cunning and beautiful work, the chapter reserving the right to reject any figure or ornament and cause it to be remade. For his work Roger was to receive the weight in silver of the shrine when completed, before gilding. No very general rule can be laid down as to the proportion between the intrinsic value or weight of metal and the cost of workmanship, but roughly in the case of simple articles of plate the cost of manufacture may be set at approximately half the weight. Thus in the case of the plate presented by the city to the Black Prince on his return from Gascony in 1371 [296] we find six chargers, weight £14, 18s. 9d., amounting with the making to £21, 7s. 2d.; twelve 'hanappes,' or handled cups, weight £8, 12s., amounting to £12, 7s. 7d.; and thirty saltcellars, weighing £15, 6s. 2d., amounting to £21, 17s. 8d. The charge for making silver basins and lavers in the same list amounts to about two-thirds of the weight. The rate appears to have remained fairly constant, as in 1416 William Randolf made four dozen chargers and eight dozen dishes of silver for King Henry V. at 30s. the pound [297].

The demand for silver plate during the later medieval period must have been brisk, for every house of any pretension had its service of plate standing on the cupboard or dresser. Nothing more astonished the Venetian travellers in England in 1500 than this extraordinary profusion and display; they noted that, [298] 'In one single street, named the Strand, are 52 goldsmiths' shops so rich and full of silver vessels, great and small, that in all the shops in Milan, Rome, Venice, and Florence put together I do not think there would be found so many of the magnificence that are to be seen in London. And these vessels are all either saltcellars or drinking-cups or basins to hold water for the hands, for they eat off that fine tin which is little inferior to silver.' Although the home of the goldsmiths is here stated to be the Strand, their chief centre was in Lombard Street and in Cheapside, where, just about the time that this Venetian account was written, Thomas Wood built Goldsmiths' Row with its ten fair houses and fourteen shops and its four-storied front adorned with allusive wild men of the wood riding on monstrous beasts [299]. Even as late as 1637 efforts were made to compel the goldsmiths to remain in Cheapside for the greater adornment of that thoroughfare [300].

The Venetian reference to the 'fine tin' used for plates and dishes serves to remind us that gold and silversmiths had no monopoly of metal-working. Pewterers, founders, and such specialised trades as bladesmiths and spurriers played an important part in the realm of industry, and if the materials upon which they worked were less valuable in themselves, the finished products were not to be despised even from a purely artistic point of view. The figures of Queen Eleanor of Castile and Henry III. , both cast by William Torel, and those of Edward III. and Queen Philippa, by Hawkin of Liége—to name but a few obvious examples—are magnificent examples of the founder's work. Mention may also be made of the tomb of Richard II. and his queen, at which Nicholas Croker and Godfrey Prest, coppersmiths, worked for four years, and for which they received £700 [301]. To deal at all fully with all the many branches of metal-working is outside the scope of this book, but two particular branches, the founding of bells and of cannon, are worth treating in considerable detail.

References to Bells [302] during Saxon times are not infrequent, but probably the earliest notice connected with their manufacture is the entry amongst the tenants of Battle Abbey in the late eleventh century of 'AEdric who cast the bells (qui signa fundebat)' [303]. It is likely that most early monastic peals were cast in the immediate neighbourhood of the monastery by, or under the supervision, of the brethren. But in the twelfth century, when Ralph Breton gave money to Rochester Cathedral Priory for a bell, in memory of his brother, the sacrist sent a broken bell up to London to be recast [304]. Possibly the craftsman who recast this bell was the Alwold 'campanarius' who was working in London about 1150 [305]. Another early bell-founder was Beneit le Seynter, sheriff of London in 1216 [306]. Mr. Stahlschmidt is no doubt right in interpreting this founder's name as 'ceinturier' or girdler, [307] for there was at Worcester in the thirteenth century a family whose members bore indifferently the name of 'Ceynturer' and 'Belleyeter' [308]. The demand for bells could hardly have been large enough to enable a craftsman to specialise entirely in that branch, and a bell-maker would always have been primarily a founder, and according as the main portion of his trade lay in casting buckles and other fittings for belts, or pots or bells, he would be known as a girdler, a potter, or a bell-founder [309].

The medieval English term for a bell-founder was 'bellyeter' (surviving in London as 'Billiter Street,' the former centre of the industry), derived from the Anglo-Saxon geotan, to pour: the word is occasionally found used independently as a verb, the agreement for casting a bell for Stansfield in 1453 stipulating that it should be 'wele and sufficiantly yette and made' [310]. So far as the process itself is concerned, [311] it remained unchanged in its main features until comparatively recent times and a considerable number of records relating to bell-founding have survived and throw a little light upon the details of the art. The first step was the formation of the 'core,' an exact model of the inside of the bell, formed of clay. When this had been hardened by baking, the 'thickness,' corresponding exactly to the projected bell itself, was built up upon the core; finally, over the 'thickness' was built a thick clay 'cope.'

Originally, it would seem, it was usual to make the 'thickness' of wax, which, melting upon the application of heat, ran out and left the space between the core and cope vacant for the molten metal to flow into: possibly some of the early uninscribed bells which still exist may have been formed in this fashion, but it seems clear that from the end of the thirteenth century the use of wax was abandoned in England, the 'thickness' being made of loam or earth [312]. The clay cope, moulded over this, was carefully raised by a crane, the 'thickness' destroyed, and the cope readjusted, after any inscription or other decoration had been stamped on its inner surface. In order that the metal might flow directly from the furnace into the mould the latter lay in a pit in front of the furnace. The furnace doors being opened, the metal, consisting of a mixture of copper and tin, flowed into the mould. If the metal was not in a sufficiently fluid state, or if any check occurred the caster would 'lose his labour and expense,' as happened to Henry Michel when he recast the great bell of Croxden Abbey in 1313, and the work would have to be done all over again [313]. But if the work had been properly carried out the completed bell had to be tuned, unless, as was the case at St. Laurence's, Reading, in 1596, 'not so much the tune of the bell was cared for as to have it a loud bell and heard far' [314].

The tuning was done by grinding, or cutting, down the rim of the bell if the note was too flat, or by reducing its thickness, filing down the inner surface of the sound bow, if the note was too sharp. In order to reduce the amount of tuning required it was necessary to know approximately the relation between size, or weight, and tone, and as early as the reign of Henry III. a monk of Evesham, Walter of Odyngton, devised a system by which each bell was to weigh eight-ninths of the bell next above it in weight [315]. This system, delightfully simple in theory, could not have yielded satisfactory results in practice, and it is probable that most founders had their own systems, based upon experience and practical observation. The question of whether a bell was correctly in tune with the others of the peal was one which naturally led to occasional disputes. When Robert Gildesburgh, brazier, of London, a fifteenth-century bell-founder, cast two bells for Whitchurch in Dorset, the vicar refused to pay for them, as he said they were out of tune. Gildesburgh requested that they should be submitted to the judgment of Adam Buggeberd, rector of South Peret, who accordingly came over and heard them rung, and decided that there was no fault in them [316]. In the case of the bells recast for the church of St. Mary-at-Hill, London, in 1510, [317] we have first an entry of 6½d. paid 'for Reves labour and his brekefast for comyng from Ludgate to Algate to here the iiij bell in tewne'; and then, as apparently the churchwardens were not satisfied with his report, 8d. paid 'for wyne and peres at Skran's howse at Algate for Mr. Jentyll, Mr. Russell, John Althorpe, John Condall and the clarkes of saynt Antonys to go and see whether smythes bell wer tewneabill or not.' Possibly the decision in the case of this fourth bell cast by William Smith was not satisfactory, as the 'great bell' seems to have been entrusted to William Culverden, a contemporary founder, many of whose bells, bearing his rebus of the culver or wood pigeon, still exist.

The bell having been fitted with an iron clapper, swung from a staple inside the crown of the bell by a leathern baudrick, was fastened on to a massive wooden stock furnished at its ends with gudgeons, or iron pivots, to work in the bronze sockets of the frame, and was now ready to be hung in the belfry. But although it was now a finished 'trade article,' there was yet one more process to be undergone before it could summon the faithful to church: it was usual, though apparently by no means universal, for the bells to be blessed. Thus the bells of St. Albans Abbey were consecrated in the middle of the twelfth century by the Bishop of St. Asaph; [318] and a detailed account of the dedication of the great bell called 'Jesus' at Lichfield Cathedral in 1477 has been preserved [319]. In the case of the five bells of St. Michael's, Bishop's Stortford, recast by Reginald Chirche of Bury St. Edmunds in 1489 at a cost of £42, an extra 17s. 6d. was paid 'for their consecration (pro sanctificacione)' [320]. That the dedication ceremony included a form analogous to baptism is clearly shown by an entry in the accounts of St. Laurence, Reading, where, in 1508, we find 'paid for hallowing the great bell named Harry 6s. 8d. And over that Sir William Symys Richard Clich and Mistress Smyth being godfather and godmother at the consecracyon of the same bell, and bearing all the costs to the suffragan' [321].

Of the early centres of the industry London was naturally the most important. Two early bell- founders of this city have already been mentioned, but it is noteworthy, as showing that to a certain extent a man might be 'jack of all trades' even if he was master of one, that several bells were cast for Westminster Abbey by Edward Fitz Odo, the famous goldsmith of Henry III [322]. That monarch, a patron of all the arts, granted 100s. yearly to the Bell-ringers' gild of Westminster for ringing the great bells [323]. Mr. Stahlschmidt has shown that the centre of the bell-founding trade was round Aldgate and in the neighbourhood of St. Andrew Undershaft and St. Botolph- without-Aldgate, [324] while amongst the more prominent early founders were the family of Wimbish at the beginning of the fourteenth century and the Burfords at the end of the same century. Contemporary with these last was William Founder, whose trade stamp, bearing his name and a representation of two birds on a conventionalised tree, occurs on a number of bells and hints at his real surname, which, although it has hitherto eluded historians, was clearly Wodeward. Mr. Stahlschmidt [325] noticed the entry on the Issue Rolls of 1385 recording the purchase of twelve cannon from William the founder, but did not notice that the very next year sixty cannon were bought from William Wodeward, [326] while in 1417 other cannon were provided by William Wodeward, founder [327].

Amongst the provincial centres we may notice Gloucester, where Hugh Bellyetare occurs about 1270, and John Belyetere in 1346, [328] the latter being presumably the Master John of Gloucester, who with his staff of six men came to Ely in 1342 to cast four bells for Prior Walsingham [329]. A later bell-founder of some eminence at Gloucester was William Henshawe, who was mayor in 1503, 1508, and 1509 [330]. Another of the craft who obtained more than local reputation was John de Stafford, mayor of Leicester in 1366 and 1370, [331] who was called in by the chapter of York to cast bells for the Minster in 1371 [332]. This is the more remarkable as York was itself a centre of the industry, the most famous of its founders being Richard Tunnoc, who represented the city in Parliament in 1327, and dying in 1330, left behind him as a worthy memorial 'the bell-maker's window' in York Minster [333]. In the central panel of this window Richard Tunnoc himself is shown kneeling before a sainted archbishop; the two other panels show the process of bell-making. In the one the master workman is supervising the flow of the metal into the mould from a furnace, the draught of which is supplied by bellows worked by two young men, the one standing upon them with one foot on each and the other holding the handles. The remaining panel is usually said to represent the moulding of the clay core, but it seems to me more likely to represent the finishing, smoothing, and polishing of the completed bell [334]. Richard Tunnoc is shown seated holding a long crooked instrument (resembling a very large boomerang), and applying it with great care to the surface of the bell, or core, which an assistant is rotating on a primitive lathe consisting of two trestles and a crooked handle. The space round each panel is filled with rows of bells swinging in trefoiled niches.

The number of churches in the larger towns being much greater in medieval times than at the present day, and few of these churches being content with a single bell, most of the chief towns, and in particular those possessing cathedrals or important monasteries, had their resident bell-founders. In the case of Exeter, Bishop Peter de Quivil, about 1285, assured the proper care of the bells of the cathedral by granting a small property in Paignton to Robert le Bellyetere as a retaining fee, Robert and his heirs being bound to make or repair, when necessary, the bells, organs, and clock of the cathedral, the chapter paying all expenses, including the food and drink of the workmen, and these obligations were duly fulfilled for at least three generations, Robert, son of Walter, son of the original Robert, still holding the land on the same terms in 1315 [335]. Canterbury was another local centre of the trade, and from Canterbury came the founder who in 1345 cast a couple of bells at Dover, the one weighing 3266 lbs., and the other 1078 lbs., for each of which he was paid at the rate of a halfpenny the pound [336]. In East Anglia there was an important foundry at the monastic town of Bury St. Edmunds, one of the fifteenth-century founders using as his trade mark a shield, which is interesting as bearing on it not only a bell, but also a cannon with a ball issuing from its mouth. Norwich, again, with its seventy churches and its cathedral priory, was a busy centre of the industry. One of the later Norwich founders, Richard Brasier, seems to have been more skilful than straightforward and to have devoted some of his skill to evading his obligations. In 1454 the churchwardens of Stansfield bargained with him to cast a bell for their church, half payment to be made on delivery and the other half at the expiration of a year and a day if the bell proved satisfactory, but if it did not he was to cast a new bell for them; he, however, taking advantage of their being unlearned men caused the latter clause to be omitted from the indenture, and when the bell proved unsatisfactory refused to make a fresh one [337]. A few years later, in 1468, the parishioners of Mildenhall brought an action against him for breach of contract. It had been agreed that the great bell of Mildenhall should be brought by the parishioners to 'the werkhous' of the said Richard Brasier and weighed by them, and that Brasier should then cast from the metal of the old bell a new tenor bell in tune with the others then in the church steeple, and should warrant it, as was customary, for a year and a day, and if it were not satisfactory should at his own expense take it back to Norwich 'to be yoten.' They had duly carried the bell to his workshop, but he had not cast it; in defence his counsel urged that although they had brought it they had not weighed it, and that until they did so he was not bound to cast it. On the other side it was argued that the point was frivolous, that he could have weighed it himself, and that indeed the indenture implied that it was to be weighed and put into the furnace by his men in the presence of the men of Mildenhall [338]. A jury was summoned, but did not appear, and the case was adjourned.

The suppression of the monasteries, followed by the seizure of Church goods, including large numbers of bells, formed the rude termination of the medieval period of the industry, and may be symbolised by the death of

William Corvehill, formerly subprior of Wenlock, 'a good bell founder and maker of the frame for bells,' at Wenlock in 1546 [339].

We have seen that a cannon is shown on the shield used as a trade mark by a fifteenth-century Suffolk bell-founder, and the casting of Ordnance may rank with the casting of bells as one of the most interesting and important branches of the founder's craft. Cannon seem to have been introduced into England at the beginning of the reign of Edward III. In 1339 there were in the Guildhall 'six instruments of latten called gonnes and five roleres for the same. Also pellets of lead weighing 4½ cwt. for the same instruments. Also 32 lbs. of powder for the same' [340]. This same year guns are recorded to have been used by the English at the siege of Cambrai, and they were also used at Creçy in 1346. Two large and nine small 'gunnes' of copper were provided for Sheppey Castle in 1365; [341] but whether any of these were of native manufacture may be doubted, though a small gun sent over to Ireland in 1360 is said to have been bought in London, [342] which does not, of course, necessarily imply that it was made there. In 1385, however, the sheriff of Cumberland included in his account of repairs to the Castle of Carlisle 'costs incurred in making three brass cannons which are in the said castle,' [343] and in the same year 'William Founder,' as we saw when considering his work as a bell-founder, provided twelve guns. Next year the same William Wodeward made no less than sixty cannon for Calais [344]. As he was still providing ordnance in 1416, [345] we may probably identify him with 'Master William Gunmaker,' who made several small cannon in 1411, two of them being of iron [346].

The early cannon were made of bronze of a similar composition to that used for bells, and when iron was introduced the cannon of that material were made in the form of a tube composed of long iron bars, arranged like the staves of a barrel, bound round with iron bands. They were all breech- loaders, consisting of two separate parts, the barrel and the chamber; the latter being a short cylinder, usually detachable, in which the charge of gunpowder was placed, and which was then fastened into the base of the barrel by means of a stirrup or similar apparatus. Double-barrelled cannon appear to have been fairly common, as in 1401 eight single cannon and six double (duplices) were sent to Dover Castle, and the same numbers to Scotland [347]. An inventory of the artillery at Berwick-on-Tweed taken at the same time [348] distinguishes between guns 'imbedded in timber bound with iron' and 'naked' guns; it also mentions 'two small brass guns on wooden sticks, called handgonnes,' an early instance of small arms. The same inventory refers to 'quarells for gonnes'; and in the previous year Henry Robertes, serjeant, dwelling near the

Guildhall, was paid £8, 8s. for twenty-four 'quarell gunnes,' [349] these being guns which threw quarrels, or bolts similar to those used with crossbows [350]. The usual projectiles employed in the larger guns were round stone balls, such as had been in use for mangonels and catapults since the days of the Romans, and these were supplied from the quarries of Maidstone and elsewhere down to the time of Henry VIII. Iron 'gunstones' do not seem to have been made much before the end of the fifteenth century, and the 'wooden balls for cannon,' of which there were 350 at Dover in 1387, [351] can hardly have proved successful, but lead was commonly employed for the smaller guns from an early date.

London was the chief centre of the manufacture of ordnance, but an iron cannon was made at Bristol in 1408, [352] and five years later John Stevenes of Bristol was ordered to supervise the making of another [353]. In 1408 'a certain great cannon newly invented by the king himself' was made; [354] this presumably was 'the great iron cannon called Kyngesdoughter,' which, shortly after its birth, was broken at the siege of 'Hardelagh' [355]. The 'Kyngesdoughter' was probably made at the Tower, as were three other iron cannon at the same time, four more being made in Southwark and two smaller ones by Anthony Gunner, possibly at Worcester as one of them was tested there and broke during the trial; of six bronze cannon made at the same time the largest, the 'Messager,' weighing 4480 lbs. and two small ones were broken at the siege of Aberystwyth. The life of a gun in those days seems to have been short, and that of a gunner precarious [356]. In 1496, when the government range was at Mile End, 13s. 4d. was given to Blase Ballard, gunner, 'towards his leche craft of his hands and face lately hurte at Myles ende by fortune shoting of a gunne,' [357] and this is not the only hint we have that these weapons were sometimes as dangerous to their users as to the enemy.

The Germans and Dutch were particularly expert in the manufacture of guns, and we find Matthew de Vlenk 'gonnemaker' in the service of Richard II., [358] while Godfrey Goykyn, one of four 'gunnemeystres' from Germany, who were serving Henry V. during the last years of his reign, [359] was employed in 1433 to finish off three great iron cannon which Walter Thomasson had begun to make [360]. These cannon threw balls of fourteen, sixteen, and eighteen inches diameter, respectively, so that presumably they were 'bombards' or mortars, and probably similar in type to one found in the moat of Bodiam Castle, and now at Woolwich; [361] the core of this specimen, which is of 15-inch calibre, is of cast-iron, the outer casing being formed of a series of bands of wrought iron, and it was probably made in

Sussex. It was in this county, at Newbridge in Ashdown Forest, that Simon Ballard in 1497 cast large quantities of iron shot, [362] those for 'bombardells' weighing as much as 225 lbs. each, so that they had to be placed in the guns by means of 'shotting cradles': [363] for 'curtows' the shot weighed 77 lbs., for 'demi-curtows' 39 lbs., for 'great serpentines' 19 lbs., and for ordinary 'serpentines' 5 lbs. This same Simon Ballard was enrolled amongst the gunners at the time of the Cornish rising under Perkin Warbeck. [364] In the same way we find 'Pieter Robard alias Graunte Pierre,' ironfounder of Hartfield, [365] described as a 'gonner,' and casting 'pellettes' at 6d. a day in 1497 [366]. In this same year ten 'faucons' (small guns which fired balls of about 2 lbs.) were made by William Frese, [367] founder, at 10s. the hundredweight, and eight faucons of brass were made by William Newport, [368] who was a London bell-founder, [369] while John Crowchard repaired an old serpentyne that John de Chalowne made and provided '10 claspis for the touche holes of diverse gonnes with 5 oliettes and fourteen staples,' weighing 53 lbs. at 2d. the pound, and also '7 bandes of yren made for the great gonnes mouthes' [370]. Cornelys Arnoldson at the same time was paid for mending five great serpentynes and making two new chambers to them, for '5 forelocks with cheynes to the said gonnes,' for 'handills made to the chambres,' and for 'vernysshing and dressing' the guns [371].

At the beginning of the reign of Henry VIII. large purchases of cannon were made abroad, from Hans Popenreuter and Lewis de la Fava of Mechlin, from Stephen of St. Iago, from Fortuno de Catalengo, and from John Cavalcante of Florence, who also, in return for a grant of alum, agreed to import saltpetre to the value of £2400 [372]. But the English foundries were not idle: Humphrey Walker, a London gunfounder, supplied fifty pieces of ordnance, at 12s. the pound, as well as much shot, [373] while Cornelys Johnson 'gonnemaker,' made and repaired ordnance for the navy [374]. John Atkynson, another founder, in 1514 was paid 2s. 'for 8 lodes of clay to make molds for a great gun chamber' and a further 8d. for 5 lbs. of hair 'to temper the clay withall'; he was also supplied with latten and iron wire, and John Dowson made certain iron work, including 'a rounde plate for the bottom of the chambre, in length 4½ feet, with 10 rounde hookes; a rounde plate with a crosse for the mouthe of the chambre; 36 bandes of 4 foot in length for to wrapp the chambre in; ... 6 pynnes of hardyron, 2 hokes, a stamme, a quespile,' etc. [375].

The medieval period of gunfounding came to an end with the discovery, about 1543, of a method of casting iron cannon in the entire piece—then boring them. This discovery is usually attributed to Ralph Hogge of Buxted and Peter Baude, his French assistant, and resulted in the ironmaking districts of the Weald of Sussex and Kent becoming the chief centre of the manufacture of ordnance [376].

Chapter 7

POTTERY—TILES, BRICKS

The manufacture of earthen vessels was one of the earliest, as it was one of the most widespread industries. From the end of the Stone Age onwards wherever suitable clay was to be found, the potter plied his trade. The Romans, who had brought the art of potting to a high pitch of excellence, introduced improved methods into Britain, where numerous remains of kilns and innumerable fragments of pottery testify to the industry and the individuality of the Romano-British potters. Several quite distinct types of pottery have been identified and are assignable to definite localities. Great quantities of black and grey wares, consisting of articles of common domestic use, ornamented for the most part only with broad bands of darker or lighter shading, were made in Kent near the Medway, the finer specimens being associated with Upchurch. From the potteries in the New Forest [377] came vases of greater ornamental and artistic execution, but it was the neighbourhood of Castor in Northamptonshire that occupied in Roman times the place held in recent times by Staffordshire. Round Castor numbers of kilns have been found, [378] and the peculiar dark ware, with its self-coloured slip decoration, occurs all over England, and also on the Continent.

Romano-British kilns have been found in a great number of places, some of the best preserved being at Castor, [379] in London, [380] at Colchester, [381] Radlett (Herts.), [382] and Shepton Mallet (Somerset) [383]. Speaking generally they consisted of a circular pit, about 4 to 6 feet in diameter, dug out to a depth of about 4 feet: in this was a flat clay floor raised some 2 feet from the bottom of the pit by a central pedestal. Into the space between this floor, or table, and the bottom of the pit came the hot air and smoke from a small furnace built at one side of the pit, or kiln proper. On the clay table, which was pierced with holes for the passage of the heat and smoke, were ranged the clay vessels to be baked, and these were built up in layers of diminishing diameter into a domed or conical structure, the layers being separated by grass covered with clay, the whole was then covered in with clay, leaving only an aperture in the centre at the top, [384] and the furnace lighted.

The early medieval kilns appear to have been very similar in construction to those just described, or of even simpler construction. If we may take literally the statement that a potter at Skipton paid 6s. 8d. in 1323 'for dead wood and undergrowth to burn round his pots' [385] it would seem that here a primitive combination of furnace and kiln in one was in use. At a later date the usual construction was probably something similar to those found at Ringmer, in Sussex, [386] which seem to belong to the fifteenth century. Here the kilns were built of bricks or blocks of clay cemented by a sandy loam which vitrified under the influence of the heat to which it was subjected. The beds of the kilns enclosed longitudinal passages covered in with narrow arches, the spaces between which served to transmit the hot air to the superimposed clay vessels. The hearths were charged through arched openings at their ends with charcoal fuel.

To render the pottery non-porous, it was necessary to glaze it, [387] and from an early period lead has been used for this purpose. A twelfth-century description of the process says [388] that the surface of the vase is first to be moistened with water in which flour has been boiled, and then powdered with lead: it is then placed inside a larger vessel and baked at a gentle heat. This process gives a yellow glaze, but if green is required—and green was the colour most often used in England in the medieval period—copper or bronze was to be added to the lead. The same authority gives a recipe for a leadless glaze: baked potter's earth is powdered and washed and then mixed with half its weight of unbaked earth, containing no sand; this is then worked up with oil and painted over the surface of the vase.

Potters are mentioned at Bladon (Oxon.), Hasfield (Gloucs.), and Westbury (Wilts.), in Domesday, [389] but apart from casual references in place names [390] and in descriptions of individuals [391] the documentary history of early English pottery is scanty. Kingston on Thames may have been an early centre of the trade, as in 1260 the bailiffs of that town were ordered to send a thousand pitchers to the king's butler at Westminster [392]. At Graffham, in Sussex, in 1341, one of the sources of the vicar's income was 'a composition from the men who made clay pots, which is worth 12d.,' [393] but the most common form of entry is a record of sums paid by potters for leave to dig clay. Thus at Cowick in Yorkshire, [394] in 1374, as much as £4,

16s. was 'received from potters making earthen vessels, for clay and sand taken in the moor of Cowick.' Similar entries occur here every year for about a century, while at Ringmer, in Sussex, small dues of 9d. a head were paid yearly by some half a dozen potters for a period of well over two hundred years. [395] Still earlier, in 1283, a rent of 36s. 8d., called 'Potteresgavel,' was paid to the lord of the manor of Midhurst [396].

The type of pottery produced does not seem to have varied to any great extent in the different districts [397]. At Lincoln it seems to have been the custom to decorate some of the vessels by means of stamps: some of these stamps, in the form of heads, may be seen in the British Museum. But the use of stamps for decorating pottery is found also at Hastings. One distinctive variety of earthenware, however, arose about the beginning of the sixteenth century: it is a thin hard pottery, dark brown in colour, well glazed, and usually decorated with elaborate patterns in white slip. From its being found in large quantities in the Cistercian abbeys of Yorkshire—Kirkstall, Jervaulx, and Fountains—it has received the name of 'Cistercian ware,' but there is at present no direct evidence of its place of manufacture [398].

Closely connected with pottery is the manufacture of Tiles, the material being in each case clay, and the kilns used being practically identical. At what period the manufacture of tiles, which had ceased with the Roman occupation, was resumed in England is not certain, but from the beginning of the thirteenth century they play an increasing part in the records of building operations. The frequency and devastating effect of fires, where thatched roofs were in use, soon led to the use of tiles for roofing purposes in towns even when the authorities did not make their use compulsory, as was done in London in 1212, and at a much later date, in 1509, at Norwich [399]. The importance, for the safety of the town, of having a large supply of tiles accessible at a low price was recognised, and in 1350, after the Black Death had sent the prices of labour and of manufactured goods up very high, the City Council of London fixed the maximum price of tiles at 5s. the thousand, [400] and in 1362, when a great tempest had unroofed numbers of houses and created a great demand for tiles, they ordered that the price of tiles should not be raised, and that the manufacturers should continue to make tiles as usual and expose them for sale, not keeping them back to enhance the price [401]. It was probably the same appreciation of the public advantage that led the authorities at Worcester in the fifteenth century to forbid the tilers to form any gild, or trade union, to restrain strangers from working in the city, or to fix a rate of wages [402].

The Worcester regulations also ordered that all tiles should be marked with the maker's sign, so that any defects in size or quality could be traced to the party responsible. Earlier in the same century, in 1425, there had been many complaints at Colchester of the lack of uniformity in the size of the tiles made there, [403] and at last it became necessary in 1477 to pass an Act of Parliament to regulate the manufacture [404]. By this Act it was provided that the clay to be used should be dug, or cast, by 1st November, that it should be stirred and turned before the beginning of February, and not made into tiles before March, so as to ensure its being properly seasoned. Care was to be taken to avoid any admixture of chalk or marl or stones. The standard for plain tiles should be 10½ inches by 6¼ inches with a thickness of at least ⅝ inch; ridge tiles or crests should be 13½ inches by 6¼, and gutter tiles 10½ inches long, and of sufficient thickness and depth. Searchers were to be appointed and paid a penny on every thousand plain tiles, a half- penny on every hundred crests, and a farthing for every hundred corner and gutter tiles examined. Infringement of the regulation entailed fines of 5s. the thousand plain, 6s. 8d. the hundred crest, and 2s. the hundred corner or gutter tiles sold. 'The size of the tiles is probably a declaration of the custom, the fine is the price at which each kind was ordinarily sold in the fifteenth century' [405]. These regulations throw a certain amount of light upon the processes employed in tile-making, and further details are obtainable from the series of accounts relating to the great tileworks in the Kentish manor of Wye, [406] extending from 1330 to 1380. In 1355 the output of ten kilns (furni) was 98,500 plain, or flat, tiles, 500 'festeux' [407] (either ridge or gutter tiles), and 1000 'corners.' The digging of the clay and burning of the kilns was contracted for at 11s. the kiln, a thousand faggots were bought for fuel [408] at a cost of 45s., and another 10s. was spent on carriage of the clay and faggots. The total expenses were therefore £8, 5s., and as plain tiles sold here for 2s. 6d. the thousand, festeux at three farthings each, and corners at 1s. 8d. the hundred, the value of the output was about £14, 15s. In 1370, when thirteen kilns belonging to two tileries turned out 168,000 plain tiles, 650 festeux, and 900 corners, we have a more elaborate account. Wood was cut at the rate of 15d. for each kiln; clay for the six kilns of one tilery was 'cast' at 14d. the kiln and 'tempered' at the rate of 1s. 6d., but for the seven kilns of the other tilery payment was made in grain. The clay was carried to the six kilns for 4s., and prepared [409] for moulding into tiles for 7s.; the actual making and burning [410] of the tiles was paid for at 14s. the kiln, and an extra 12d. were given as gratuities to the tilers. Next year the output was considerably reduced, because in one tilery 'the upper course of the kilns (cursus furni) did not bake the tiles fully, nor will it bake them until extensive repairs are done,' and in the other tilery only four kilns were prepared, and one of these had to be left unburnt until the next year, owing to the lack of workmen. It was possibly for the defective kiln just mentioned that a 'new vault' was made in 1373 at a cost of 6s. 8d.—with a further 8d. for obtaining loam (limo) for the work. Two years later repairs were done to the buildings of a tilery, which had been blown down by the wind. But the chief blow was struck to the industry here by the increasing difficulty of obtaining workmen. The work may have been unhealthy, for it is noteworthy that the Ringmer potters were on more than one occasion wiped out by pestilence: [411] the effects of the Black Death in 1350 on the Wye tilers are not recorded, but in 1366 as a result, apparently, of the second pestilence two small tileries, one of three roods, and the other of 1½ acres, which had been leased for 7d. and 14d. respectively, lost their tenants, and in 1375 mention is made of the scarcity of workmen, 'who died in the pestilence at the time of tile making.' In 1377 Peter at Gate, [412] who for the past few years had hired a number of kilns at 20s. a piece, only answered for four kilns 'on account of hindrance to the workmen, who had been assigned to guard the sea coast, and on account of the great quantity of rain in the autumn, which did not allow him to burn more kilns.' In the same year, and also two years later, another tilery was unworked for lack of labour.

The tileries at Wye belonged to the Abbot of Battle, and there were tile kilns at Battle itself in the sixteenth century, [413] and probably much earlier, as in the adjoining parish of Ashburnham in 1362, there was a 'building called a Tylehous for baking (siccandis) tiles.' [414] Just about the same time, in 1363, we find 'a piece of land called Teghelerehelde' in Hackington, [415] close to Canterbury, granted to Christian Belsire, in whose family it remained for over a century, as in 1465 William Belsyre leased to John Appys and Edmund Helere of Canterbury 'a tyleoste with a workhouse' lying at Tylernehelde in Hackington for two years for a rent of 26s. 8d [416]. With the 'tyleoste' William Belsyre handed over 15,000 'tyle standardes'—worth 18d. the thousand, eighty 'palette bordes and three long bordys for the kelle walles' [417]. Various building accounts show that there were extensive tileries at Smithfield; for Guildford Castle the tiles came from Shalford, and for Windsor chiefly from 'la Penne.' In the north tiles were made before the end of the thirteenth century at Hull, amongst other places, but one of the chief centres was Beverley. About 1385 the monks of Meaux complained that 'certain workmen of Beverley who were called tilers, makers and burners of the slabs (laterum) with which many houses in Beverley and elsewhere are covered,' had trespassed on the abbey's lands at Waghen and Sutton, taking away clay between the banks and the stream of the river Hull without leave, to convert into tiles. The monks seized their tools, their oars, and finally one of their boats, but the Provost of Beverley, on whose fee the tileries were, supported the tilers in their claim to dig clay in any place covered by the waters of the Hull at its highest [418]. Some thirty years earlier, in 1359, the list of customary town dues at Beverley included 'from every tiler's furnace fired ½d.,' [419] and in 1370 Thomas Whyt, tiler, took a lease of the tilery of Aldebek from the town authorities for four years, at a rent of 6000 tiles [420].

So far we have been dealing with roofing tiles, or 'thakketyles,' but from the middle of the fourteenth century onwards with increasing frequency, we find mention of 'waltyles' or bricks. For building a new chamber at Ely in 1335 some 18,000 wall tiles (tegularum muralium) were made at a cost of 12d. the thousand. [421] They seem to have been introduced from Flanders, and are frequently called 'Flaundrestiell,' [422] as, for instance, in 1357, when a thousand were bought for a fireplace at Westminster at 3s. 2d. [423]. At Beverley, in 1391, three persons acquired from the gild of St. John the right to take earth at Groval Dyke, paying yearly therefor 3000 'waltyles,' [424] and in 1440 Robert Collard, tile-maker, took 'le Grovaldyke on the west side of le demmyng' at a rent of 1000 'waltyl' [425]. It was probably more particularly with regard to brick kilns than to ordinary tile kilns that the regulations drawn up in 1461 [426] ordered that, 'on account of the stench, fouling the air and destruction of fruit trees, no one is to make a kiln to burn tile nearer the town than the kilns now are, under penalty of a fine of 100s.' The term 'brick' does not seem to have come into common use much before 1450, about which time the use of the material became general.

In addition to roof tiles and wall tiles, there were floor tiles. References to these occur in many building accounts. At Windsor, in 1368, 'paven-tyll' cost 4s. the thousand, and a large variety 2s. the hundred, while plain roof tiles were 2s. 6d. the thousand [427]. These were probably plain red tiles, but at Westminster in 1278 we have mention of the purchase of 'a quarter and a half of yellow tiles' for 7d. [428]. Tiles with a plain yellow or green glazed surface are of common occurrence in medieval buildings, and in many churches and monastic ruins pavements of inlaid, so-called 'encaustic,' tiles remain more or less complete [429]. In the case of these inlaid tiles the pattern was impressed or incised before baking, and then filled in with white slip, the whole being usually glazed. Some of the patterns thus produced were of great beauty and elaboration, and it would seem that they were often designed, if not actually made, by members of monastic houses. The finest known series are those discovered at Chertsey Abbey, and it is possible that the remarkable examples in the chapter-house of Westminster Abbey, [430] which date from c. 1255, are by the same artist. In the case of the Abbey of Dale in Derbyshire, [431] and the priories of Repton and Malvern, [432] the kilns used for making these inlaid tiles have been discovered, and similar kilns, not associated, so far as is known, with any religious establishment, have also been found at Hastings [433]. The manufacture of these inlaid tiles in England gradually died out towards the end of the fifteenth century, and has only been revived in recent years.

It is curious that although there is abundant circumstantial evidence of Glassmaking in England, during the medieval period, direct records of the manufacture are extremely scarce, and practically confined to a single district. From the early years of the thirteenth century, Chiddingfold and the neighbouring villages on the borders of Surrey and Sussex were turning out large quantities of glass. Laurence 'Vitrarius' (the glassman) occurs as a landed proprietor in Chiddingfold about 1225, and some fifty years later there is a casual reference to 'le Ovenhusfeld,' presumably the field in which was the oven or furnace house, of which the remains were uncovered some years since. [434] It is possible that in the case of glassmaking, as in the case of many other industries, improvements were introduced from abroad, for in 1352 we find John de Alemaygne [435] of Chiddingfold supplying large quantities of glass for St. Stephen's Chapel, Westminster [436]. In one batch he sent up three hundred and three weys (pondera) of glass, the wey being 5 lbs. , and the hundred consisting of twenty-four weys, being, that is to say, the 'long hundred' of 120 lbs. A little later he sent thirty-six weys, and soon after another sixty weys were bought at Chiddingfold, probably from the same maker. The price in each case was 6d. the wey, or 12s. the hundred, to which had to be added about 1d. the wey for carriage from the Weald to Westminster. In January 1355-6 four hundreds of glass were bought from the same maker for the windows of St. George's Chapel, Windsor, at 13s. 4d. the hundred [437].

Towards the end of the fourteenth century the family of Sherterre, or Shorter, became prominent in the Chiddingfold district, [438] and on the death of John Sherterre in 1380 his widow engaged John Glasewryth, of Staffordshire, to work the glass-house for six years, receiving 20d. for every sheaf (sheu) [439] of 'brodeglass' (i.e., window glass), and 6d. for every hundred of glass vessels made. This is interesting as showing that glass vessels were made here; the evidence of inventories, however, seems to show that glass was as a whole very little used for table purposes, though a few pieces of the beautiful Italian glassware might be found in the houses of the wealthy. The family of Shorter were succeeded by the Ropleys, and they in turn by the Peytos, who carried on the trade during the whole of the sixteenth century, and as late as 1614, thus well overlapping the modern period of glassmaking, which began with the coming of the gentilshommes verriers from France early in the reign of Elizabeth [440].

Glass must have been made in many other districts where fuel and sand, the chief requisites for the manufacture, were plentiful, but it is difficult to identify any sites of the industry. In 1352 John Geddyng, glazier, was sent into Kent and Essex to get glass for St. Stephen's, Westminster, [441] but where he went and whether he was successful, is not known. 'English glass' is found in use at Durham in 1397, [442] and at York in 1471 [443]. For York Minster sixteen sheets (tabulae) of English glass were bought from Edmund Bordale of Bramley buttes for 14s. 8d. in 1478, [444] and at an earlier date, in 1418, we find three seams, three weys of white glass bought from John Glasman of Ruglay (Rugeley) at 20s. the seam of twenty-four weys, [445] but whether these men were glass makers, or merely glass merchants, cannot be determined. That the industry, so far at least as real stained glass is concerned, was not flourishing in England in the fifteenth century is shown by the fact that Henry VI. , in 1449, brought over from Flanders John Utynam to make glass of all colours for Eton College and the College of St. Mary and St. Nicholas (i.e., King's) Cambridge. He was empowered to obtain workmen and materials at the King's cost, and full protection was granted to him and his family. He was also allowed to sell such glass as he made at his own expense, and 'because the said art has never been used in England, and the said John is to instruct divers in many other arts never used in the realm,' the King granted him a monopoly, no one else being allowed to use such arts for twenty years without his licence under a penalty of £200 [446]. Most glass of which we have any account was bought through the glaziers of the larger towns; but to what extent they made their own glass we cannot say. A certain amount, especially of coloured glass, was imported, and the York accounts show 'glass of various colours' bought in 1457 from Peter Faudkent, 'Dochman' (i.e., German), at Hull, [447] 'Rennysshe' glass bought in 1530, Burgundy glass in 1536, and Normandy glass in 1537, [448] while in 1447 we find the executors of the Earl of Warwick stipulating that no English glass should be used in the windows of his chapel at Warwick [449].

To any one who knows the beauty of English stained glass this stipulation may seem strange, but it must be borne in mind that our cathedral windows derive their glories not from the maker, but from the painter, and that the glass is but the medium carrying the designs of the artist. English glass as a rule, prior at any rate to the fifteenth century, was white and received its decoration after it had left the glass-house. The process may be gathered from the account of St. Stephen's in 1352. Here we find John of Chester and five other master glaziers employed at a shilling a day drawing designs for the windows on 'white tables,' presumably flat wooden tablets, which were washed with ale, [450] which served no doubt as a size or medium to prevent the colours running. About a dozen glaziers were employed at 7d. a day to paint the glass, and some fifteen, at 6d. a day, to cut or break the glass and join it, [451] which they apparently did by placing it over the painted designs, this being presumably done before it was painted. The glass thus cut into convenient shapes was held in place over the design by 'clozyngnailles,' and when it had been painted was joined up with leads, lard or grease being used to fill the joints. For the painting silver foil, gum arabick, jet (geet), and 'arnement' (a kind of ink) were provided [452]. Possibly the stronger colours were supplied by the use of pieces of stained glass, as purchases were made of ruby, azure, and sapphire glass.

Chapter 8

CLOTHMAKING

Important as was the wool trade, for centuries the main source of England's wealth, its history, pertaining to the realms of commerce rather than of industry, does not concern us here, and we may ignore the raw material to deal with the manufactured article. To treat at all adequately the vast and complicated history of clothmaking would require a volume as large as this book, even if the line be drawn at the introduction of the New Draperies by Protestant refugees in the time of Elizabeth, and all that is possible here is briefly to outline that history.

The weaving of cloth is of prehistoric antiquity, implements employed therein having been found in numbers in the ancient lake-village of Glastonbury, and on other earlier sites, but documentary evidence may be said to begin with the twelfth century. By the middle of that century the industry had so far developed in certain centres that the weavers of London, Winchester, Lincoln, Oxford, Huntingdon, and Nottingham, and the fullers of Winchester, had formed themselves into gilds, which were sufficiently wealthy to pay from 40s. to £12 yearly to the king for various privileges which practically amounted to the monopoly of cloth-working in their several districts [453]. If these were the principal they were by no means the only centres of the industry. Stamford, [454] on the borders of Lincolnshire and Northants, was another; and Gloucester, [455] while dyers are found at Worcester [456] in 1173, and at Darlington [457] ten years later.

To the twelfth century also belong the remarkable 'laws of the weavers and fullers' of Winchester, Marlborough, Oxford, and Beverley. [458] These, which all closely resemble one another, and were either based upon, or intimately related to the regulations in force in London, show the clothworkers in a state of subjection for which it is difficult to account. Briefly summarised, they lay down that no weaver or fuller may traffic in cloth or sell it to any one except to the merchants of the town, and that if any became prosperous and wished to become a freeman of the town, he must first abandon his trade and get rid of all the implements connected with it, and then satisfy the town officials of his ability to keep up his new position without working at his old trade. But the most singular provision, found in all these laws, was that no fuller or weaver could attaint or bear witness against a 'free man.' Here it is clear that 'free man' is used not as opposed to a villein, [459] but as implying one possessing the full franchise of his town, in other words, a member of the governing merchant gild, or equivalent body. Probably the English cloth trade, which was very extensive during the twelfth century, was entirely in the hands of the capitalist merchant clothiers, at any rate so far as the great towns here in question were concerned, and they had combined to prevent members of the handicraft gilds of clothworkers from obtaining access to the merchant gilds. As the charter granted to the London weavers by Henry II. early in his reign confirms to them the rights and privileges which they had in the time of Henry I., and orders that no one shall dare to do them any injury or despite, [460] it may be suggested that these restrictive regulations were drawn up in the time of Stephen. For the date at which they were collected, evidently as precedents for use in London, we may hazard 1202, in which year the citizens of London paid sixty marks to King John to abolish the weavers' gilds [461].

It is curious that most modern writers assume the English cloth trade to have practically started with the introduction of Flemish weavers by Edward III. It is constantly asserted [462] that prior to this the cloth made in England was of a very poor quality and entirely for home consumption. Both statements are incorrect. A very large proportion of the native cloth was certainly coarse 'burel,' such as that of which 2000 ells were bought at Winchester in 1172 for the soldiers in Ireland, [463] or the still coarser and cheaper Cornish burels which were distributed to the poor by the royal almoner about this time [464]. At the other end of the scale were the scarlet cloths for which Lincoln and Stamford early attained fame. Scarlet cloth, dyed if not actually made on the spot, was bought in Lincoln for the king in 1182 at the prodigious price of 6s. 8d. the ell, about £7 in modern money. At the same time 'blanket' cloth and green say cost 3s. the ell, and grey say 1s. 8d [465]. Thirty years later the importance of the trade is indicated by the inclusion in Magna Carta of a section fixing the breadth of 'dyed cloths, russets, and halbergetts' at two ells 'within the lists' [466]. Infringements of the 'assize of cloth' were of constant occurrence, and were amongst the matters inquired into by the justices holding 'pleas of the Crown'; for instance, in Kent, in 1226, some thirty merchants and clothiers are presented as offenders in this respect, [467] Henry III. at the beginning of his reign, in May 1218, had ordered that any cloths of less than two ells breadth exposed for sale should be forfeited, [468] but this order was not to take effect before Christmas so far as burels made by the men of London, Marlborough, and Bedwin (Wilts.) were concerned, and in 1225 the citizens of London were exempted from keeping the assize, provided their burels were not made narrower than they used to be [469]. In 1246 the sheriff of London was ordered to buy one thousand ells of cheap burel to give to the poor; [470] and in 1250 we find the king discharging an outstanding bill of £155 due to a number of London burellers, whose names are recorded; [471] amongst them was one Gerard le Flemeng, but otherwise they appear to have been native workmen. The burellers seem to have already separated off from the weavers, and had certainly done so some time before 1300, at which date disputes between the two classes of clothmakers were common [472].

Apart from the burels, which were probably very similar wherever made, the cloths made at different centres usually possessed distinctive characteristics. In the list of customs paid at Venice on imported goods in 1265, [473] we find mention of 'English Stamfords,' 'dyed Stamfords,' and of 'Milanese Stamfords of Monza,' showing that this particular class of English cloth was sufficiently good to be copied abroad. It is rather a noticeable feature of the cloth trade that so many of the trade terms were taken from the names of the places in which the particular wares originated. A prominent instance of this occurs in the case of 'chalons,' which derived their name from Chalons-sur-Marne, but were made in England from an early date. 'Chalons of Guildford' were bought for the king's use at Winchester Fair in 1252 [474]. Winchester itself was an early centre of the manufacture of chalons, which were rugs used for coverlets or counterpanes, and in the consuetudinary of the city, [475] which dates back at least to the early years of the thirteenth century, the looms are divided into two classes, the 'great looms' used for burel weaving paying 5s. a year, and the 'little looms' for chalons paying 6d. or 12d., according to their size. The chalons were to be of fixed dimensions, those 4 ells long being 2 yards in breadth (devant li tapener), those of 3½ yards 1¾ yards wide, and those of 3 ells long 1½ ells wide. Coverlets formed also an important branch of the Norfolk worsted [476] industry; in this case the ancient measurements were said in 1327 to have been 6 ells by 5, 5 by 4, or 4 by 3 [477]. At a later date, in 1442, we find worsted 'beddes' of much greater dimensions, the three 'assizes' being 14 yards by 4, 12 by 3, or 10 by 2½,

[478] but presumably these were complete sets of coverlet, tester and curtains, such as those of which a number are valued at from 6s. 8d. to 20s. a piece in the inventory of the goods of the late King Henry V. in 1423 [479]. Besides bedclothes the worsted weavers made piece cloth, and amongst the exports from Boston in 1302 figure worsted cloths and worsted seys [480]. Boston, as we might expect from its nearness to Lincoln, exported a good deal of scarlet cloth, while the amount of 'English cloth' sent out is proof of a demand for this material abroad: a ship from Lubeck took 'English cloth' worth £250 for one merchant, Tideman de Lippe, and two other ships carried cargoes of the same material worth more than £200. 'Beverley cloths' are also represented amongst these exports, and coloured cloths of Lincoln and Beverley are found about this time at Ipswich paying the same tolls as foreign cloths. [481] At Ipswich also cloths of Cogsall, Maldon, Colchester, and Sudbury are mentioned as typical 'clothes of Ynglond' exported [482] and are classified as 'of doubele warke that men clepeth tomannyshete,' and a smaller kind 'of longe webbe that they call omannesete,' [483] or 'oon mannys hete.' The origin of these terms appears to be unknown, but as these were probably the narrow cloths afterwards known as 'Essex straits,' there was possibly some connection with the narrow 'Osetes' of Bristol [484].

So far as London is concerned, the skill of the weavers at the end of the thirteenth century is shown by the variety of types of cloth which are referred to in the regulations of 1300 [485]. Here we find mention of cloths called andly, porreye, menuet, virli, lumbard, marbled ground with vetch- blossom, hawes, bissets, etc. But it would seem that the English cloth makers failed to keep pace [486] with their Continental rivals, and instead of improving the quality of their goods endeavoured to keep up prices by restricting their output [487]. Edward III., seeing the need for new blood, took measures to attract foreign clothworkers [488] to England, and at the same time, in 1337, absolutely prohibited the use or importation of foreign cloth [489]. In order to stimulate the output he even withdrew all restrictions as to measures, and licensed the making of cloths of any length and breadth; but this excess of freedom soon proved unworkable. The newcomers were not very popular with the native weavers, and in 1340 the king had to send orders to the Mayor of Bristol to cease from interfering with Thomas Blanket and others who had set up machines for making cloth, and had brought over workmen [490]. The vexation against which Blanket had appealed seems to have been the regulation that every new weaving loom was to pay 5s. 1d. to the Mayor, and 40d. to the aldermen; this rule was confirmed in 1346, but annulled in 1355 [491].

Before dealing with the various ordinances by which the manufacture of cloth was controlled, it may be as well to consider the processes through which the wool passed before it reached the market, for 'Cloth that cometh from the weaving is not comely to wear Till it be fulled under foot or in fulling stocks; Washen well with water, and with teasels cratched, Towked and teynted and under tailor's hands' [492].

Having dropped into verse, we may perhaps continue in that medium, and set out the various stages of the manufacture in a poem, [493] written in 1641, but equally applicable to earlier times:—

1. First the Parter, that doth neatly cull
   The finer from the courser sort of wool [494].
2. The Dyer then in order next doth stand,
   With sweating brow and a laborious hand.
3. With oil they then asperge it, which being done,
4. The careful hand of Mixers round it runne.
5. The Stockcarder his arms doth hard imploy
   (Remembring Friday is our Market day).
6. The Knee-carder doth (without controule)
   Quickly convert it to a lesser roule.
7. Which done, the Spinster doth in hand it take
   And of two hundred roules one threed doth make.
8. The Weaver next doth warp and weave the chain,
   Whilst Puss his cat stands mewing for a skaine;
   But he, laborious with his hands and heeles,
   Forgets his Cat and cries, Come boy with queles [495].
9. Being fill'd, the Brayer doth it mundifie
   From oyle and dirt that in the same doth lie,
10. The Burler [496] then (yea, thousands in this place)
    The thick-set weed with nimble hand doth chase.
11. The Fuller then close by his stock doth stand,
    And will not once shake Morpheus by the hand.
12. The Rower next his armes lifts up on high,
13. And near him sings the Shearman merrily.
14. The Drawer last, that many faults doth hide
    (Whom merchant nor the weaver can abide)
    Yet is he one in most clothes stops more holes
    Than there be stairs to the top of Paul's.'

The first process, then, was the sorting of the wool. The better quality was used for the ordinary cloths, and the worst was made up into coarse cloth known as cogware and Kendal cloth, three- quarters of a yard broad, and worth from 40d. to 5s. the piece [497]. The term cogware seems to have sprung from its being sold to cogmen, the crews of the ships called cogs; but whether for their own use, or for export is not quite clear. The alternative name of Kendal cloths was derived from the district of Kendal in Westmoreland, a seat of the industry, at least as early as 1256 [498]. The mixing of different qualities of wool in one cloth was prohibited; and as it was forbidden to mix English wool with Spanish, [499] so was the use of flocks, or refuse wool, in ordinary cloth, [500] except in the case of the cloth of Devonshire, in which, owing to the coarseness of the wool, an admixture of flock was necessary [501].

In dyeing two mediums are required, the colouring matter and the mordant which fixes the dye in the wool. The mordant most in use in the Middle Ages was alum, [502] and at Bristol in 1346 we find that only 'Spyralym, Glasalym, and Bokkan' might be used and that any one using 'Bitterwos' or 'Alym de Wyght,' which must have derived its name from the Isle of Wight, or even found with any in his possession, was liable to be fined [503]. Far the commonest dye-stuff was the blue woad, of which enormous quantities were used. The plant (Isatis tinctoria) from which this was prepared is indigenous (the ancient Britons, indeed, wore the dye without the intervention of cloth), but practically all the woad used commercially in England was imported, Southampton being one of the great centres of the trade [504]. In 1286 the authorities at Norwich came to an agreement with the woad merchants of Amiens and Corby as to the size of the packages in which woad and weld, a yellow dye in much demand, might be sold, [505] and at Bristol some sixty years later elaborate regulations were drawn up for the preparation of the woad, of which two varieties are mentioned, that of Picardy and that of Toulouse [506]. The woad was imported in casks in the form of dry balls; these had to be broken up small, moistened with water, and then heaped up to ferment; after a few days the top layer became so hot that it could hardly be touched with the hand; the heap was then turned over to bring the bottom to the top, and left till this in turn had fermented; a third turn usually sufficed to complete the process [507]. In Bristol special 'porters' were appointed to undertake and supervise this seasoning and the subsequent storing of the woad, and a further regulation compelled the merchant to sell his woad within forty days after it had been stored and assayed [508]. The setting of the woad, that is to say its conversion into dye, was also an art in itself, and it would seem that in Bristol it was the custom for dyers to go to the houses of their customers and prepare the woad-vats. Through undertaking more jobs than they could properly attend to, much woad was spoilt, and in 1360 they were forbidden to take charge of more than one lot of dye at one time [509]. Further abuses arose through the ignorance and incapacity of many of the itinerant dyers, and in 1407 it was enacted that only those dyers who held a certificate of competency should ply their trade in the town [510]. At Coventry, another great centre of the trade, complaints were made in 1415 that the dyers had not only raised their prices, charging 6s. 8d. instead of 5s. for a cloth, 30s. instead of 20s. for 60 lbs. of wool, and 6s. instead of 4s. for 12 lbs. of the thread for which the town was famous, but were in the habit of taking the best part (la floure) of the woad and madder for their own cloths, and using only the weaker portion for their customers' cloths. A petition was therefore made that two drapers, a woader and a dyer, should be elected annually to supervise the trade [511]. Some fifty years later we have at Coventry a notice of what appears to have been a medieval instance of a quarrel between a 'trade union,' the Dyers Company, and 'blackleg' firms [512]. Thomas de Fenby and ten other dyers of Coventry complained against John Egynton and William Warde that they had assembled the members of their trade and had compelled them to swear to various things contrary to the law and their conscience, as that no one should buy any woad until it had been viewed and appraised by six men chosen for the purpose by the said Egynton and Warde, and that no dyer should make any scarlet dye (grene) at less than 6s. (the vat?), or put any cloth into woad for less than 4d. or 5d. Warde and Egynton had also adopted the medieval form of picketing, by hiring Welshmen and Irishmen to waylay and kill the complainants on their way to neighbouring markets.

A list of cloths made in York in 1395-6 [513] gives some idea of the colours in general use. For the first three months, September-December, blue largely predominated, but for some unexplained reason this colour almost disappeared from January to May, its place being taken by russet. Red, sanguine, morrey (or orange), plunket, [514] green, and motleys, white, blue, and green occur; also 'paly,' which was presumably some striped material, and in a very few cases black. By the regulations drawn up in London in 1298, [515] no dyer who dyed burnets blue [516] or other colours might dye 'blecche' or tawny: the reason does not appear, but this uncertain tint, 'blecche,' occurs again as reserved specially for Spanish wool [517]. For blue, as we have seen, woad was used, and for yellow weld, a combination of the two yielding green; scarlet was derived from the grain (greyne), [518] and reds and russets from madder, which was imported in large quantities. Several varieties of lichen were probably included under the head of 'orchal,' and afforded shades of brown and red. Fancy shades were formed by double dyeing, and apparently were not always reliable, as a statute [519] passed in 1533 ordered that none should dye woollen cloth 'as browne blewes, pewkes, tawnyes, or vyolettes,' unless they were 'perfectly boyled, greyned, or madered upon the wode, and shotte with good and sufficient corke or orchall.' At this time brazil, or logwood, was being adopted as a dye, and its use was absolutely forbidden.

Carding, or combing, and spinning are processes which need not detain us long. They were both home industries, and spinning, in particular, was the staple employment of the women, and accordingly regulations were not infrequently made to ensure a good supply of wool for their use. At Bristol, in 1346, no oiled wool ready for carding and spinning might be sent out of the town until the carders and spinners had had a chance of applying for it; moreover, it might only be exposed for sale on a Friday, and no middleman might buy it [520]. Similarly at Norwich, in 1532, the butchers were ordered to bring their woolfells into the market and offer them for sale to the poor women who lived by spinning [521]. When the clothmaking trade got into the hands of the big capitalist clothiers, who gave out their wool to be carded and spun, it became necessary to pass laws [522] to ensure on the one hand that the workers should do their work faithfully, and not abstract any of the wool, [523] and on the other, that the masters should not defraud the carders and spinners by paying them in food or goods [524] instead of in money, or by the use of false weights, making women, for instance, comb 7½ lbs. of wool as a 'combing stone,' which should only contain 5 lbs [525].

Weaving was, of course, the most important of all the processes in clothmaking. Reduced to its simplest form, the weaver's loom consists of a horizontal frame, to the ends of which the warp threads, which run longitudinally through the cloth, are fastened in such manner that they can be raised and depressed by heddles, or looped threads, in alternate series, leaving room between the two layers of warp for the passage of the shuttle, charged with the woof [526]. The shuttle, flying from side to side across the alternating warp threads, covers them with woof, which is packed close by a vertical frame of rods, the lay or batten, swinging between the warp threads. To weave tight and close required considerable strength, and at Norwich women were forbidden to weave worsteds because they were 'not of sufficient power' to work them properly [527]. The cloth as it was woven was wound on a roll, bringing a fresh portion of the warp within the weaver's reach, but while its length was thus limited merely by custom or convenience, its breadth was obviously controlled by the width of the loom, and when Henry IV. , in 1406, ordered that cloth of ray should be made six-quarters of a yard broad instead of five-quarters, as had always been the custom, the order had to be revoked as it would have necessitated all the ray weavers obtaining new looms [528]. For the right to use looms payments had often to be made to authorities of the town. At Winchester in the thirteenth century, every burel loom paid 5s. yearly, the only exceptions being that the mayor, the hospital, and the town clerk might each work one loom free of charge [529]. Nottingham was another town where duties were paid on looms, [530] and at Bristol, as we have seen, prior to 1355, the erection of a 'webanlam' entailed payments of 8s. 5d. in all.

To guard against false working, it was the rule at Bristol that all looms must stand in shops and rooms adjoining the road, and in sight of the people, and the erection of a loom in a cellar or upstair room entailed a fine [531]. It was possibly for the same reason that weavers were forbidden to work at night, [532] though an exception was made at Winchester in favour of the period immediately preceding Christmas [533]. On the other hand, the London jurors in 1320 coupled this ordinance against working by candle light with the enforced holiday which the weavers' gild compelled its members to take between Christmas and the Purification (2nd February) [534] as measures prejudicial to the commonalty, and intended to restrict the supply and so maintain the price of cloth [535]. A further device for the same purpose was the rule that no cloth of Candlewick Street was to be worked in less than four days, though they might easily be made in two or three days [536]. Thanks to these methods, and to the way in which admission to the gild was limited, the looms in the city had been reduced in thirty years or so from 380 to 80, and the price of cloth had risen accordingly. The authorities throughout the country were constantly in the dilemma of having on the one hand to permit the restriction of the numbers of the weavers, with a consequent rise in the cost of their wares, or, on the other hand, running the risk of inferior workmanship 'to the grete infamie and disclaundre of their worshipfull towne.' Not only were the unauthorised weavers often ignorant of their art, not having served their apprenticeship, but they used flock and other bad material, and bought stolen wool and 'thrummes' [537]. The latter were the unwoven warp threads left over at the end of the cloth, and as there was no export duty on thrums, the weavers contrived to cut them off as long as possible, and in this way much woollen yarn was sent out of the country without paying customs, until the practice was made illegal by an Act of Parliament in 1430 [538].

The cloth on leaving the loom was in the condition known as 'raw,' and although not yet ready for use was marketable, and many of the smaller clothmakers preferred to dispose of their products at this stage rather than incur the expense of the further processes. This seems to have been the case on the Welsh border, as Shrewsbury claimed to have had a market for ' pannus crudus ' from the time of King John [539]. Much raw cloth was also bought up by foreign merchants and sent out of the country to be finished; and at the beginning of the sixteenth century Parliament, with its usual terror of foreign trade, seeing only that the finishing processes would be carried out by foreign workmen instead of English, forbade the export of unfinished cloth. It had then to be pointed out that, as most of these cloths were bought to be dyed abroad, and as after dyeing all the finishing processes would have to be repeated, the cost of the cheaper varieties would be so raised that there would be no sale for them; cloths below the value of five marks were therefore exempted [540].

Raw cloth had next to be fulled, that is to say, scoured, cleansed, and thickened by beating it in water. Originally this was always done by men trampling upon it in a trough, and the process was known as 'walking,' the fuller being called a 'walker' (whence the common surname), but during the thirteenth century an instrument came into general use called 'the stocks,' consisting of an upright, to which was hinged the 'perch' or wooden bar with which the cloth was beaten. The perch was often worked by water power and fulling, or walking, mills soon became common. By the regulations of the fullers' gild of Lincoln recorded in 1389, [541] no fuller was to 'work in the trough,' that is to say to walk the cloth, and a further rule forbade any man to work at the perch with a woman, unless she were the wife of a master or her handmaid. Probably the intention of this last rule was to put a stop to the employment of cheap female labour 'by the whiche many ... likkely men to do the Kyng servis in his warris and in the defence of this his lond, and sufficiently lorned in the seid crafte, gothe vagaraunt and unoccupied and may not have thar labour to ther levyng.' [542] About 1297 a number of London fullers took to sending cloths to be fulled at certain mills in Stratford, and as this was found to result in much loss to the owners of the cloths, orders were given to stop all cloths on their way to the mills, and only allow them to be sent on at the express desire of the owners [543]. This seems to point to mill fulling being inferior to manual labour, while possibly the fulling being conducted outside the control of the city may have tended to bad work. At Bristol in 1346, one of the rules for the fullers forbids any one to send 'rauclothe' to the mill, and afterwards receive it back to be finished, [544] and in 1406 the town fullers were forbidden to make good the defects in cloths fulled by country workmen [545].

For cleansing the cloth use was made of the peculiar absorbent earth known as Fuller's earth, or 'walkerherth,' [546] as it was sometimes called. Fuller's earth is only found in a few places, the largest deposits being round Nutfield and Reigate, [547] and on account of its rarity and importance its export was forbidden.

The cloth, having been fulled, had to be stretched on tenters to dry, and references to the lease of tenter grounds are common in medieval town records. [548] A certain amount of stretching was legitimate and even necessary, [549] but where the cloth belonged to the fuller, and it was a common practice for fullers to buy the raw cloth, there was a temptation to 'stretch him out with ropes and rack him till the sinews stretch again' [550] so as to gain several yards. As a result of this practice, which greatly impaired the strength of the cloth, 'Guildford cloths,' made in Surrey, Sussex, and Hampshire, lost their reputation, and in 1391 measures had to be taken to restore their good name by forbidding fullers, or other persons, to buy the cloth in an unfinished state [551]. Several other Acts were passed dealing with this offence, and during the sixteenth century ordinances were issued against the use of powerful racks with levers, winches, and ropes. Infringements of these Acts were numerous, [552] and as an example of the extent to which cloths were stretched we may quote a return from Reading in 1597, which mentions one cloth of thirty yards stretched with 'a gyn and a leaver with a vice and a roape' to thirty-five yards, and another stretched with a rope 'to the quantitye of three barrs length—every barr contayneth about 2½ yards' [553].

On leaving the fuller the cloth passed into the hands of the rower, whose business it was to draw up from the body of the cloth all the loose fibres with teazles. Teazles, the dried heads of the 'fuller's thistle,' are mentioned amongst the goods of some of the Colchester cloth-workers in 1301, [554] were used from the earliest times, and have never been supplanted even in these days of machinery. Several unsuccessful attempts have been made to invent substitutes, and in 1474 the use of iron cards, or combs, instead of teazles, had to be forbidden [555]. The loose portions of the cloth thus raised by the teazles were next cut off by the shearman, upon whose dexterity the cloth depended for the finish of its surface, and, after the drawer had skilfully repaired any small blemishes, the cloth was ready for sale.

In view of the multiplicity of processes involved, it is obvious that the manufacture of cloth must have afforded employment to an immense number of persons. An account written in Suffolk just over the borders of our medieval period, in 1618, reckons that the clothier who made twenty broad cloths in a week would employ in one way and another five hundred persons [556]. But even at that time, when the capitalist clothier was firmly established, there were not very many with so large an output as twenty cloths a week, and in earlier times there were very few approaching such a total. The ulnager's accounts [557] of the duties paid on cloths exist for most counties for the last few years of Richard II. , and throw considerable light on the state of the trade. In the case of Suffolk for the year 1395, we have 733 broad cloths made by about one hundred and twenty persons, of whom only seven or eight return as many as twenty cloths; the chief output, however, was narrow cloth, made in dozens (pieces of 12 yards, a 'whole cloth' being 24 yards); of these 300 makers turned out about 9200, fifteen of their number making from 120 to 160 dozens each. In the case of Essex there is more evidence for the capitalist clothier, as at Coggeshall the 1200 narrow cloths are assigned to only nine makers (the largest items being 400, 250, and 200 dozens), while Braintree, with 2400 dozens had only eight makers, of whom two pay subsidy on 600 dozens each and one on 480. The great clothiers, however, at this time are found in the west, at Barnstaple, where John Parman paid on 1080 dozen, and Richard Burnard on 1005, other nine clothiers dividing some 1600 dozens between them. For the rest of Devonshire, sixty-five makers account for 3565 dozens, or rather over fifty a piece. If Devon stood at one end of the scale its next-door neighbour was at the other, for Cornwall's total output was only ninety cloths, attributed to thirteen makers. At Salisbury the year's output of 6600 whole cloths was divided between 158 persons, only seven of whom accounted for more than 150 each, while at Winchester, where over 3000 cloths are returned, only three clothiers exceeded the hundred, and men of such local prominence as Robert Hall and 'Markays le Fayre' [558] had only eighty and forty to their respective accounts. Throughout Yorkshire the average does not seem to have been above ten cloths, and in Kent, a stronghold of the broad cloth manufacture, only one clothier exceeded fifty dozens, and only three others passed twenty-five. The whole evidence seems to limit the spheres of influence of the capitalist clothiers to a few definite towns prior to the beginning of the fifteenth century. But the latter half of the fifteenth century saw the rise of the great clothiers such as John Winchcombe, [559] the famous 'Jack of Newbury,' and the Springs of Lavenham, [560] employers of labour on a scale which soon swamped the small independent clothworkers, and drew them into a position of dependence.

Skill and industry in the cloth trade had always been assured of a good return, and when combined with enterprise had often led to wealth; but there have always in all times and all places been men who would try the short cut to fortune through fraud; and the openings for fraud in the cloth trade were particularly numerous. 'Certayne townes in England ... were wonte to make theyre clothes of certayne bredth and length and to sette theyre seales to the same; while they kept the rate trulye strangers dyd but looke over the seale and receyve theyre wares, wherebye these townes had greate vente of theyre clothes and consequently prospered verye welle. Afterwards some in those townes, not content with reasonable gaynes but contynually desyrynge more, devysed clothes of lesse length, bredthe and goodnes thanne they were wonte to be, and yet by the comendacioun of the seale to have as myche monye for the same as they had before for good clothes. And for a tyme they gate myche and so abused the credythe of theyr predecessours to theyre singulere lukere, whiche was recompensede with the losse of theyre posterytye. For these clothes were founde fawltye for alle theyre seale, they were not onelye never the better trustede but myche lesse for theyre seale, yea although theyre clothes were well made. For whanne theyr untruth and falshede was espyede than no manne wolde buye theyre clothes untylle they were enforsede and unfoldede, regardynge nothynge the seale' [561].

This complaint, written in the time of Henry VIII. , is borne out in every detail by the records of Parliament and of municipalities. Regulations were constantly laid down for ensuring uniformity, and officials called ulnagers [562] were appointed to see that they were obeyed, no cloth being allowed to be sold unless it bore the ulnager's seal. The assize of cloth issued in 1328 [563] fixed the measurements of cloth of ray at 28 yards by 6 quarters, and those of coloured cloths at 26 yards by 6½ quarters, in the raw state, each being 24 yards when shrunk. The penalty for infringement of the assize was forfeiture [564]. This assize, which was confirmed in 1406, repealed next year, but reaffirmed in 1410, [565] applied only to broad cloths, but in 1432 it was laid down [566] that narrow cloths called 'streits' should be 12 yards by 1 yard, when shrunk; if smaller they were not forfeited, but the ulnager cut the list off one end, to show that it was not a whole cloth, and it was sold as a 'remnant' according to its actual measure. In the case of the worsteds or serges of Norfolk, four different assizes were said in 1327 to have been used from time immemorial, namely, 50, 40, 30, and 24 ells in length; [567] but as early as 1315 merchants complained that the cloths of Worsted and Aylesham did not keep their assize, 20 ells being sold as 24, 25 ells as 30, and so on [568]. In the western counties, Somerset, Gloucester, and Dorset, fraudulent makers were in the habit of so tacking and folding their cloths that defects in length or quality could not be seen, with the result that merchants who bought them in good faith and took them to foreign countries were beaten, imprisoned and even slain by their angry customers 'to the great dishonour of the realm.' It was therefore ordered in 1390 that no cloth should be sold, tacked, and folded, but open [569]. The frauds in connection with stretching Guildford cloths have already been referred to, and in 1410 we find that worsteds which had formerly been in great demand abroad were now so deceitfully made that the Flemish merchants were talking of searching, or examining, all the worsted cloths at the ports of entry. To remedy this 'great slander of the country,' the mayor and his deputies were given the power to search and seal all worsteds brought to the worsted seld, or cloth market, and regulations were made as to the size of 'thretty elnys streites' (30 ells by 2 quarters), 'thretty elnys brodes' (30 ells by 3 quarters), 'mantelles, sengles, doubles et demy doubles, si bien les motles, paules, chekeres, raies, flores, pleynes, monkes-clothes et autres mantelles' (from 6 to 10 ells by 1¼ ell), and 'chanon-clothes, sengles, demy doubles et doubles' (5 ells by 1¾), the variety of trade terms showing the extent of the industry [570]. A similar complaint of the decay in the foreign demand for worsteds owing to the malpractices of the makers was met in 1442 by causing the worsted weavers of Norwich to elect annually four wardens for the city, and two for the county to oversee the trade [571]. Half a century later, in 1473, English cloth in general had fallen into disrepute abroad, and even at home, much foreign cloth being imported: to remedy this general orders were issued for the proper working of cloth, the maintenance of the old assize, and the indication of defects, a seal being attached to the lower edge of any cloth where there was any 'raw, skaw, cokel or fagge' [572].

The last-mentioned statutes of 1473 give the measurements of the cloths as by the 'yard and inch.' Originally it would seem to have been customary when measuring cloth to mark the end of each yard by placing the thumb on the cloth at the end of the clothyard, and starting again on the other side of the thumb. Readers of George Eliot will remember that the pedlar, Bob Salt, made ingenious use of his broad thumb in measuring, to the detriment of his customers; and the London drapers in the fifteenth century claimed to buy by the 'yard and a hand,' marking the yards with the hand instead of with the thumb, and thereby scoring two yards in every twenty-four [573]. Although this was forbidden in 1440, the use being ordered of a measuring line of silk, 12 yards and 12 inches long, the end of each yard being marked an inch, it evidently continued in practice, as the 'yarde and handfull' was known as London measure at the end of the sixteenth century [574].

The last years of the medieval period of the woollen industry, which we take as terminating with the introduction of the 'New Draperies' by foreign refugees early in the reign of Elizabeth, are chiefly concerned with the rise of the town clothiers at the expense of the small country cloth workers, assisted by Acts which restricted, or at least aimed at restricting, the industry to corporate boroughs and market towns, and prohibited any from setting up in trade without having passed a seven years' apprenticeship [575]. Infringements of these laws were frequent, and, thanks to the system of granting a portion of the fines inflicted to the informer, accusations were constantly levelled against clothiers for breaking the various regulations with which the trade was hedged about [576]. Many of the charges fell through, and in some cases they look like blackmail, but that offences were sufficiently plentiful is clear. For the one year, 1562, as many as sixty clothiers from Kent alone, mostly from the neighbourhood of Cranbrook and Benenden, were fined for sending up to London for sale cloths deficient in size, weight, quality, or colour [577]. An absolute fulfilment of all the regulations was possibly no easy thing, for although cloths which had been sealed by the ulnager in the district where they were made were not supposed to pay ulnage in London the makers preferred as a rule to pay a halfpenny on each cloth to the London searchers rather than risk the results of too close a scrutiny [578].

Of the many local varieties of cloth made in England that which derived its name from the village of Worsted in Norfolk was, on the whole, the most important. We have seen that by the end of the thirteenth century worsted weaving was well established in Norfolk, and particularly in Norwich, and that worsted serges and says were articles of export, while a century later the forms in which these cloths were made up were very varied. Norwich continued to hold the monopoly of searching and sealing worsteds, wherever made, until 1523, when the industry had grown to such an extent in Yarmouth that the weavers of that town were licensed to elect a warden of their own to seal their cloth; the same privilege was granted to Lynne, provided there were at least ten householders exercising the trade there; but in all cases the cloths were to be shorn, dyed, coloured, and calendered in Norwich [579]. When the art of calendering worsteds, that is to say giving them a smooth finish by pressing, was introduced in Norwich is uncertain, but in the second half of the fifteenth century the 'fete and misterie of calendryng of worstedes' in London was known only to certain Frenchmen. An enterprising merchant, William Halingbury, brought over from Paris one Toisaunts Burges, to teach the art to English workers, and, in revenge, one of the London French calenders endeavoured to have Halingbury arrested on his next visit to Paris [580]. At the beginning of the sixteenth century a process of dry calendering with 'gommes, oyles and presses' was introduced, by which inferior worsteds were made to look like the best quality, but if touched with wet they at once spotted and spoiled. The process was therefore prohibited in 1514, and at the same time the practice of wet calendering was confined to those who had served seven years' apprenticeship, and had been admitted to the craft by the mayor of Norwich or the wardens of the craft in the county of Norfolk [581].

In 1315 cloths of Aylsham (in Norfolk) are coupled with those of Worsted as not conforming to the old assize, [582] and at the coronation of Edward III. some 3500 ells of 'Ayllesham' was used for lining armour, covering cushions and making 1860 pennons with the arms of St. George [583]. But as Buckram and Aylsham are constantly bracketed together, [584] being used, for instance, in 1333 for making hobby horses (hobihors) for the king's games, [585] presumably at Christmas, it would seem that Aylshams were linen and not woollen, especially as 'lynge teille de Eylesham' was famous in the fourteenth century [586].

In the adjacent county of Suffolk the village of Kersey was an early centre of clothmaking, and gave its name to a type of cloth which was afterwards made in a great number of districts. The kerseys of Suffolk and Essex were exempted in 1376, with other narrow cloths, from keeping the assize of coloured cloths, [587] and just a century later the measurement for kerseys was set out as 18 yards by 1 yard [588]. Curiously enough the chief trouble with the assize of kerseys, at least in the sixteenth century, was not short measure, but over long, the explanation being that kerseys paid export duty by the whole cloth, and it was therefore to the merchant's advantage to pay duty on a piece of 25 yards rather than to pay the same duty on 18 yards [589]. Kerseys were largely made for export, and a petition against restrictions tending to hamper foreign trade was presented, about 1537, by the kersey weavers of Berks., Oxford, Hants, Surrey, and Sussex, and Yorkshire [590]. These counties were the chief centres of the manufacture, though Devonshire kerseys were also made; in Berkshire, Newbury was then the great seat of the industry, and the kerseys of John Winchcombe ('Jack of Newbury') in particular had a more than local fame. Hampshire kerseys was the generic name applied to these made in Hampshire, Sussex, and Surrey, but in earlier times the Isle of Wight had almost a monopoly of the manufacture in the district. The ulnage accounts for Hampshire in 1394-5 give ninety names of clothiers for the Isle of Wight, [591] who made 600 kerseys, and no other kind of cloth, and about a century later we find a draper complaining that when he had bargained with a London merchant for a certain number of 'kersys of Wyght' worth £6 he had been put off with Welsh kerseys worth only £4, 13s. 4d. [592].

Suffolk did a considerable trade in a cheap, coarse variety of cloth known as 'Vesses or set cloths' for export to the East; and, as it was the recognised custom to stretch these to the utmost, and they were bought as unshrunk, this class of cloth was exempted in 1523 from the regulations as to stretching cloth [593]. Possibly these Vesses were connected with the 'Western Blankett of Vyse (Wilts.) and Bekinton.' [594] Blanket is found in 1395 as made at Maldon and, on the other side of England, at Hereford, while at an earlier date, in 1360, Guildford blanket was bought for the royal household [595]. As Norwich had its 'monk's cloth' and 'canon cloth,' presumably so called from its suitability for monastic and canonical habits, unlike the fine cloth of Worcester, which, we are told, was forbidden to Benedictines, [596] so we find that the newly made knight of the Bath had to vest himself in 'hermit's array' of Colchester russet [597]. Most of the cloths made in Essex were 'streits,' or narrow cloths, of rather a poor quality, being often coupled with the inferior cloths such as cogware and Kendal cloth. Of the latter a writer of the time of Henry VIII. says, 'I knowe when a servynge manne was content to goo in a Kendall cote in sommer and a frysecote in winter, and with playne white hose made meete for his bodye.... Now he will looke to have at the leaste for Somere a cote of finest clothe that may be gotten for money and his hosen of the finest kerseye, and that of some straunge dye, as Flaunders dye or Frenche puke, that a prynce or a greate lorde canne were no better if he were [wear] clothe' [598].

By the sumptuary law of 1363 farm labourers and others having less than 40s. in goods were to wear blanket and russet costing not more than 12d. the ell [599]. In a list of purchases of cloth in 1409, narrow russet figures at 12d. the ell, while of the other cheap varieties short blanket, short coloured cloth, rays, motleys and friezes varied from 2s. to 2s. 4d. the ell [600]. Of friezes the two chief types in use were those of Coventry and Irish friezes, which might either be made in Ireland or of Irish wool: these seem to have come into use about the middle of the fourteenth century, as in 1376 Irish 'Frysseware' was exempted from ulnage, [601] and about the same time purchases of Irish frieze for the royal household become more common, as much as nearly 3000 ells of this material being bought in 1399 [602].

With such local varieties as Manchester cottons, Tauntons, Tavistocks, Barnstaple whites, Mendips, 'Stoke Gomers alias thromme clothes,' [603] and so forth, space does not permit of our dealing, while by the limitation which we have set ourselves the 'new draperies' are excluded, and we may thankfully leave on one side 'arras, bays, bewpers, boulters, boratoes, buffins, bustyans, bombacyes, blankets, callimancoes, carrells, chambletts, cruell, dornicks, duraunce, damask, frisadoes, fringe, fustyans, felts, flanells, grograines, garterings, girdlings, linsey woolseyes, mockadoes, minikins, mountaines, makerells, oliotts, pomettes, plumettes, perpetuanas, perpicuanas, rashes, rugges, russells, sattins, serges, syettes, sayes, stamells, stamines, scallops, tukes, tamettes, tobines, and valures' [604].

Chapter 9

LEATHER WORKING

The dressing of skins and preparation of leather must have been one of the most widely diffused industries in medieval times, even if it is a little exaggeration to claim that it was a by-product of most villages [605]. Two different processes were employed, ox, cow, and calf hides being tanned by immersion in a decoction of oak bark, while the skins of deer, sheep, and horses were tawed with alum and oil, and the two trades were from early times kept quite separate, tanners and tawyers being forbidden to work skins appropriated to each other's trade. A certain concentration of the industry must have been brought about in 1184, when orders were issued that no tanner or tawyer should practise his trade within the bounds of a forest except in a borough or market town, [606] the object being to prevent the poaching of deer for the sake of their skins. Market towns had the further advantage of being well supplied with the raw material, as butchers were compelled to bring the hides of their beasts into market with the meat, and the tanners had the sole right of purchase, no regrater or middle-man being allowed to intervene, while on the other hand the tanners were not allowed to buy the hides outside the open market [607]. Towards the end of the sixteenth century it was said [608] that 'in most villages of the realm there is some one dresser or worker of leather, and ... in most of the market towns three, four, or five, and many great towns 10 or 20, and in London and the suburbs ... to the number of 200 or very near.' Casting back, we find at Oxford in 1380 there were twelve tanners, twenty skinners, twelve cordwainers, or shoemakers, and four saddlers, [609] while in 1300 there were at Colchester forty householders employed in the various branches of the leather trade [610].

Originally, no doubt, the leather dresser worked up his own leather, and as late as 1323 it would seem that at Shrewsbury cordwainers were allowed to tan leather, [611] but in 1351 the tanners and shoemakers were definitely forbidden to intermeddle with each other's craft, and a series of regulations, parliamentary and municipal, served to separate the tanners, the curriers, who dressed and suppled the rough tanned hides, the tawyers, and the various branches of leather- workers.

The stock in trade of the tanner was simple. The inventories of the goods of half a dozen tanners at Colchester in 1300 are identical in kind though varying in value; [612] each consists of hides, oak bark, and a number of vats and tubs. In the case of the tannery at Meaux Abbey [613] (the larger monastic houses usually maintained their own tanneries) in 1396 rather more details are given. There were in store cow and calf leather, 'sole peces, sclepe, clowthedys, and wambes' to the value of £14, 10s. 4d., 15 tubs and various tools, such as 3 'schapyng-knyfes' and 4 knives for the tan; 400 tan turves (blocks of bark from which the tan had been extracted), and 'the tan from all the oaks barked this year.' The raw hides had first to be soaked, then treated with lime to remove the hair, and then washed again before being placed in the tan vat. Consequently leather- dressers settled 'where they may have water in brooks and rivers to dress their leather; without great store of running water they cannot dress the same' [614]. In 1461 William Frankwell, when making a grant of a meadow at Lewes, reserved the right to use the ditch on the south side of the meadow for his hides, [615] and complaints of the fouling of town water supplies by leather workers were not unusual [616]. The process of tanning was, and for the best leather still is, extremely slow; the hides were supposed to lie in the 'wooses' (ooze, or liquor) for a whole year, and stringent regulations were issued to prevent the hastening of the process, to the detriment of the leather. The bark from which the tan was obtained, and which was so important a feature of the process that 'barker' was an alternative name for tanner, had to be only of oak, the use of ash bark being forbidden; nor might lime or hot liquor be used, the imbedding of the vats in hot beds of old tan being prohibited.

Hides, both raw and tanned, ranked with cloth as a leading article of trade, both home and foreign; [617] and, like cloth, tanned leather was early subject to examination by searchers, appointed either by the craft gild or by the town authorities. As a rule the searcher's seal was affixed in the market, or at the particular 'seld' or hall where alone leather might be sold, but at Bristol in 1415 the searchers were empowered to examine the hides at the curriers' houses before they were curried [618]. The curriers, whose business it was to dress the 'red' hides with tallow, [619] rendering them smooth and supple, were not allowed to dress badly tanned hides [620]. Several grades of tanning were recognised, the most lengthy and thorough workmanship being required for leather intended for the soles of boots and rather less for the uppers. When forty- seven hides belonging to Nicholas Burle, of London, were seized in 1378 as not well tanned, he admitted that they were not fit for shoeleather, but urged that he intended to sell them to saddlers, girdlers, and makers of leather bottles: a mixed jury of these various trades, however, condemned the hides as unfit for any purpose, and they were forfeited [621].

Although there was thus an efficient control exercised over tanned leather, the tawed soft leathers used by glovers, pointmakers, pursemakers, saddlers, girdlers, coffermakers, budgetmakers, stationers, etc., seem for the most part to have escaped supervision, with the result that at the end of the sixteenth century the markets were flooded with counterfeit leathers [622].

'All Tawed leather is dressed with
{
Oil, as
{ Buff Shamoys
}
of the first and best sort.

{
or with Alum and Oker as the hides of
{
Horse, Stag, Hind, Buck, Doe, Calf, Dog, Seal, Sheep, Lamb, Kid.

'The leather dressed with oil is made more supple, soft and spongey, and is wrought with a rough cotton, as bayes and fresadoes are, the cotton being raised in the fulling mill where cloth is fulled, and serveth for the more beauty and pleasure to the wearer.

'The leather dressed with alum and oker is more tough and "thight," serving better for the use of the poor artificer, husbandman, and labourer, and a more easy price by half, and is wrought smooth or with cotton which is raised by hand with a card or other like tool, and as the alum giveth strength and toughness, the oker giveth it colour, like as the oil doth give colour to Buff and Shamoys.

'And this diversity of dressing, with oil or alum, is to be discerned both by smell and by a dust which ariseth from the alum leather....

'All Shamoys leather is made of goat skins brought for the most part out of Barbury, from the "Est countries," Scotland, Ireland, and other foreign parts, unwrought, and is transported again being wrought. And there is much thereof made from skins from Wales and other parts within the realm.... Being dressed with oil it beareth the name Shamoys, but being dressed with alum and oker, it beareth not the name or price of Shamoys, but of Goat skins.'

'Shamoys [623] is made of goat, buck, doe, hind, sore, sorrell, and sheepskins. The true way of dressing is in "trayne oyle," the counterfeit is with alum and is worth about half.... Shamoys dressed in train oil can be dressed again three or four times, and seem as good as new, but dressed in alum it will hardly dress twice and will soon be spied. And when Shamoys dressed in alum cometh to the rain or any water they will be hard like tanned leather, and Shamoys in oil make the cheapest and most lasting apparel, which the "low countrie man and the highe Almayn" doth use.'

Frauds in the preparation and sale of leather were of frequent occurrence, and in 1372 the mayor and aldermen of London ordained penalties for the sale of dyed sheep and calf leather scraped and prepared so as to look like roe leather. At the same time the leather dyers were forbidden to dye such counterfeit leathers, and also to use the brasil or other dye provided or selected by one customer for the goods of another [624]. With the same object of preventing frauds the tawyers who worked for furriers were not allowed to cut the heads off the skins which they dressed, and were also liable to imprisonment if they worked old furs up into leather [625]. Further penalties for false and deceitful work, especially in the making of leather 'points and lanyers,' or laces and thongs, were enacted in 1398 [626]. With the growth of capitalism during the reign of Elizabeth the control exercised by the Leathersellers' Company became almost nominal, some half a dozen wealthy members of the company getting the whole trade into their own hands. By buying up the leather all over the country, they forced up prices; having, moreover, a practical monopoly of tawed leathers they were able to make the glovers and other leather workers take the dressed skins in packets of a dozen, which contained three or four small 'linings' or worthless skins [627]. They also undertook the dressing of the skins, and cut out the good workmen by scamping their work and employing men who had only served half their seven years' apprenticeship [628]. They also caused dogskins, 'fishe skynnes of zeale,' calf, and other skins to be so dressed as to resemble 'right Civill (i.e., Seville) and Spannish skynnes,' worth twice as much. These skins were dressed 'with the powder of date stones and of gaule and with French shomake that is nothinge like the Spannish shomake, to give them a pretie sweete savor but nothinge like to the civile skynnes, and the powder of theise is of veary smale price and the powder of right Spannish shomake grounded in a mill is wourth xxx s the c lb weight, which shomake is a kynd of brush, shrubb, or heath in Spayne and groweth low by the ground and is swete like Gale [629] in Cambridgshire and is cutt twise a yeare and soe dried and grounded into powder by milles and dresseth all the Civile and Spannish skynnes brought hither' [630]. To remedy these frauds there was a general demand that tawed leather should be searched and sealed in the same way as tanned, and in 1593 Edmund Darcy turned this to his own advantage by obtaining a royal grant of the right to carry out such searching and sealing. This was opposed by the leather-sellers, on the grounds that it would interfere with the sale and purchase in country districts if buyer and seller had to wait till the searcher could attend, and that the proposed fees for sealing were exorbitant, amounting to from a ninth to nearly a half of the value of the skins. They also said that if a seal were put on, it would almost always be pared away, washed out, or 'extincte by dying' before the leather reached the consumer [631]. Upon examination the suggested fees were found to be too large, and a table of the different kinds of leather and their values was drawn up, and fees fixed accordingly: [632] —

White Tawed
Value
Fee

Sheep skins
7s.—3s. the doz.
2d., 1d.

Kid and fawn
4s. 6d.—1s. 8d. "
2d., 1d.

Lambs
4s. 4d.—1s. 8d. "
2d., 1d.

Horse [633]
5s.—2s. 6d. each
2d.

Dogs
4s.—1s. 6d. the doz.
2d., 1d.

Bucks
4s.—3s. 4d. each
8d. the doz.

Does
2s. 4d.—1s. 8d. "
8d. "

Calf
12s.—4s. the doz.
6d., 3d.
Goat
2s. 6d. each—3s. 6d. the doz.
6d., 2d. each.

Oil Dressed
Value
Fee

Right Buffe [634]
33s. 4d.—15s. each
7d.

Counterfeit Buffe
13s. 4d.—7s. "
7d.

Right Shamoise
30s. the doz.
7d.

Counterfeit"
14s."
7d.

Sheep "
8s. "
3½d.

Lamb "
6s. "
3½d.

Right Spannish skins [635]
30s."
7d.

Counterfeit Spannish skins of goat and buck
3 li."
7d.

Counterfeit Spannish sheep skins
12s."
3½d.

Right Cordovan skins
40s."
12d.

Seal skins dressed
40s."
7d.

Stagge skins, [636] English, Scottish, as big as buffyn, dressed like buffe
12s. each
6d.

Stag skins, Irish, dressed like buffe
3 li. the doz.
12d.

Buck and doe, dressed like buffe
40s. "
12d.

Calf skins, in like sort
16s. "
7d.

A number of trades, such as glovers, saddlers, pursemakers, girdlers, and bottlemakers, used leather, but the most important class were the shoemakers. They in turn were divided into a number of branches, at the head of which stood the cordwainers, who derived their name from having originally been workers of Cordovan leather, but were in actual practice makers of the better class of shoes [637]. At the other end were the cobblers, or menders of old shoes. Elaborate regulations were made in London in 1409 to prevent these two classes trespassing on one another's preserves [638]. The cobbler might clout an old sole with new leather or patch the uppers, but if the boot required an entirely new sole, or if a new shoe were burnt or broken and required a fresh piece put in, then the work must be given to the cordwainer. A distinction was also drawn at a much earlier date, in 1271, [639] between two classes of cordwainers, the allutarii and the basanarii , the latter being those who used 'basan' or 'bazan,' an inferior leather made from sheepskin. Neither was to use the other's craft, though the allutarius might make the uppers (quissellos) of his shoes of bazan: to prevent any confusion the two classes were to occupy separate positions in the fairs and markets. In 1320 we find eighty pairs of shoes seized from twenty different persons, thirty-one pairs being taken from Roger Brown of Norwich, and forfeited for being made of bazan and cordwain mixed [640]. Fifty years later, in 1375, a heavy fine was ordained for any one selling shoes of bazan as being cordwain, [641] and a similar ordinance was in force at Bristol in 1408 [642]. By the London rules of 1271, no cordwainer was to keep more than eight journeymen (servientes), and at Bristol in 1364 the shoemakers were restricted to a single 'covenant-hynd,' who was to be paid 18d. a week and allowed eight pairs of shoes yearly. [643] In the case of Bristol, however, no limit is stated for the number of journeymen, who were paid by piecework, the rates being, in 1364, 3d. a dozen for sewing, and 3d. for yarking; 3d. for making a pair of boots entirely, that is to say, 1d. for cutting and 2d. for sewing and yarking; 2d. for cutting a dozen pairs of shoes, namely 1d. for the overleathers and 1d. for the soles, and a further 1d. for lasting the dozen shoes. The rates of pay were still the same in 1408, though there are additional entries of 12d. for sewing, yarking, and finishing a dozen boots and shoes called 'quarter-schone,' and 7d. for sewing and yarking, with an extra 1½d. for finishing a dozen shoes called 'course ware' [644].

The sale of the finished articles was also an object of regulations: in London in 1271, shoes might only be hawked in the district between Corveiserstrete and Soperes Lane, and there only in the morning on ordinary days, though on the eves of feast they might be sold in the afternoon [645].

Leather laces also might not be sold at the 'eve chepings.' [646] Possibly it was considered that bad leather might be more easily passed off in a bad light, but the idea may simply have been to prevent the competition of the pedlars and hawkers with the shopkeepers. At Northampton, in 1452, the two classes of tradesmen were separated, those who had shops not being allowed to sell also in the market [647]. Northampton had not at this date begun to acquire the fame which it earned during the seventeenth century as the centre of the English boot trade, but regulations for the 'corvysers crafte' there had been drawn up in 1402, [648] and much earlier, in 1266, we find Henry III. ordering the bailiffs of Northampton to provide a hundred and fifty pairs of shoes, half at 5d. and half at 4d. the pair [649]. These were for distribution to the poor; and similar orders in other years were usually executed in either London or Winchester: no particular importance can be attached to this single order being given to Northampton, as presumably any large town could have carried out the order. So far as any town can be placed at the head of the shoemaking industry, the distinction must be given to Oxford where the cordwainers' gild was in existence early in the twelfth century, it being reconstituted in 1131, [650] and its monopoly confirmed by Henry II [651].

Chapter 10

BREWING—ALE, BEER, CIDER

Malt liquors have been from time immemorial the national drink of England, but the ale of medieval times was quite different from the liquor which now passes indifferently under the names ale or beer. It was more of a sweet wort, of about the consistency of barley water. Andrew Borde, [652] writing in the first half of the sixteenth century, says: 'Ale is made of malte and water; and they the which do put any other thynge to ale than is rehersed, except yest, barme or godesgood, doth sofysticat theyr ale. Ale for an Englysshe man is a naturall drynke. Ale must have these propertyes: it muste be fresshe and cleare, it muste not be ropy nor smoky, nor must it have no weft nor tayle. Ale should not be dronke under v dayes olde. Newe ale is unholsome for all men. And sowre ale, and dead ale the which doth stand a tylt, is good for no man. Barly malte maketh better ale then oten malte or any other corne doth: it doth ingendre grose humoures; but yette it maketh a man stronge.'

The supremacy of English ale was already established by the middle of the twelfth century, that of Canterbury being particularly famous, [653] and casks of ale were amongst the presents taken by Becket to the French court on the occasion of his embassy in 1157 [654]. At this time it really deserved the title of 'the people's food in liquid form'; the consumption per head of population must have been enormous, the ordinary monastic corrody, or allowance of food, stipulating for a gallon of good ale a day, with very often a second gallon of weak ale. It must be borne in mind that it was drunk at all times, taking the place not only of such modern inventions as tea and coffee, but also of water, insomuch that a thirteenth-century writer describing the extreme poverty of the Franciscans when they first settled in London (A.D. 1224) exclaims, 'I have seen the brothers drink ale so sour that some would have preferred to drink water' [655]. Such was the importance attached to ale that it was coupled with bread for purposes of legal supervision, and the right to hold the 'assize of bread and ale' was one of the earliest justicial privileges asserted by municipal and other local courts. The Assize of Ale as recorded on the Statute Rolls in the time of Henry III. fixed the maximum price of ale throughout the kingdom on the basis of the price of malt, or rather of the corn from which malt was made [656]. When wheat stood at 3s. or 3s. 4d. the quarter, barley at 20d. to 2s., and oats at 16d., then brewers in towns were to sell two gallons of ale for a penny, and outside towns three or four gallons. And when three gallons were sold for a penny in a town then four gallons should be sold for a penny in the country. If corn rose a shilling the quarter, the price of ale might be raised a farthing the gallon [657]. A later ordinance, issued in 1283, set the price of the better quality of ale at 1½d.; and that of the weaker at 1d., and the commonalty of Bristol, fearing that they might be punished if the brewers of the town broke this regulation, issued stringent orders for its observance, infringement entailing the forfeiture of the offender's brewery [658].

A very casual examination of court rolls and other local records is sufficient to convince the student that brewing was universal, every village supplying its own wants, and that infringements of the regulations by which the trade was supposed to be controlled were almost equally universal. The same names are found, where any series of rolls exists, presented at court after court for breaking the assize in one way or another, and it is clear that a strict observance of the laws was difficult, it being more profitable to break them and pay the small fines extorted practically as licensing dues. At Shoreham in the thirteenth century, the brewers, whose trade was particularly active because of the numbers of foreigners who visited the port, paid 2½ marks yearly to escape the vexations of the manorial court, [659] and in the same way the hundred of Shoyswell (in Sussex) paid a yearly fine in order that the ale-wives (trade was largely in the hands of women) might be excused attendance at the law-days [660]. In neither case, however, can we suppose that the manorial control over the brewing trade was appreciably relaxed, but rather that personal attendance at the court, with its interruption of business, was dispensed with. Besides these monetary payments, there were often payments in kind due to the lord of the manor or borough. At Marlborough every public brewery had to pay to the constable of the castle from each brew a measure, known as 'tolsester,' prior to 1232, when this render of ale was granted to the canons of St. Margaret's [661]. 'Tolsester' was also paid to the castle of Chester, [662] and in Newark and Fiskerton [663]. The 'sester' (sextarius) or 'cestron' was, in Coventry at any rate, 13 or 14 gallons [664]. Ale was always supposed to be sold, whether in gross or retail, in measures of which the capacity had been certified by the seal or stamp of the official appointed for the purpose [665]. The list of standard measures kept at Beverley in 1423 shows a potell, quart, pint, and gill of pewter, panyers, hopir, modius, firthindal, piece, and half-piece of wood and a gallon, potell, third and quart, also of wood [666]. Court Rolls, however, show that the use of unstamped measures and the retailing of ale in pitchers and jugs (per ciphos et discos) was of constant occurrence, [667] mainly, no doubt, for the convenience of customers who brought their own jugs, but also occasionally with intent to deceive, as in the case of Alice Causton, [668] who in 1364 filled up the bottom of a quart measure with pitch and cunningly sprinkled it with sprigs of rosemary, [669] for which she had to 'play bo pepe thorowe a pillery.' It is interesting to notice that at Torksey in 1345, if a woman was accused of selling ale 'against the assize,' she might clear herself by the oaths of two other women, preferably her next-door neighbours [670].

When a public brewer had made a fresh brew he had to send for the official 'ale-conner' or 'taster,' or to signify that his services were required by putting out in front of his house an 'ale stake,' a pole with a branch or bush at the end: this was also used as the universal sign of a tavern; and some of the London taverners, possibly recognising that their liquor was not sufficiently good to 'need no bush,' made their ale-stakes so long as to be dangerous to persons riding in the street [671]. No ale might be sold until it had been approved by the ale-conner. If the latter found the ale fit for consumption but not of full quality, he might fix the price at which it might be sold [672]. In Worcester the instructions to the ale-conner were, 'You shall resort to every brewer's house within this city on their tunning day and there to taste their ale, whether it be good and wholesome for man's body, and whether they make it from time to time according to the prices fixed. So help you God' [673]. There seems reason for the pious ejaculation when we find that in Coventry in 1520 there were in a total population of 6600 men, women, and children, 60 public brewers [674]. When the ale was good the task must have had its compensations, but when it was bad the taster must often have wished to make the punishment fit the crime, as was done in the case of a Londoner who sold bad wine, the offender being compelled to drink a draught of the wine, the rest of which was then poured over his head [675]. Our sympathy may in particular be extended to the ale- tasters of Cornwall, where 'ale is starke nought, lokinge whyte and thycke, as pygges had wrasteled in it' [676]. Oddly enough we find mention in Domesday Book of forty-three cervisiarii at Helstone in

Cornwall; they are usually supposed to be tenants who paid dues of ale, but the term is clearly used in the description of Bury St. Edmunds for brewers. In the sixteenth century, however, Borde [677] in an unflattering dialect poem makes the Cornishman say:—

> 'Iche cam a Cornyshe man, ale che can brew; It wyll make one to kacke, also to spew;
> It is dycke and smoky, and also it is dyn;
> It is lyke wash as pygges had wrestled dryn.'

To ensure the purity of the ale not only was the finished product examined, but some care was taken to prevent the use of impure water, regulations to prevent the contamination of water used by brewers, or the use by them of water so contaminated, being common [678]. On the other hand, owing to the large quantities of water required for their business, they were forbidden in London, [679] Bristol, [680] and Coventry [681] to use the public conduits. For the actual brewing, rules were also laid down. In Oxford in 1449, in which year nine brewers were said to brew weak and unwholesome ale, not properly prepared, and not worth its price, but of little or no value, the brewers were made to swear that they would brew in wholesome manner so that they would continue to heat the water over the fire so long as it emitted froth, and would skim the froth off, and that after skimming the new ale should stand long enough for the dregs to settle before they sent it out, Richard Benet in particular undertaking that his ale should stand for at least twelve hours before he sent it to any hall or college [682]. In London also casks when filled in the brewery were to stand for a day and a night to work, so that when taken away the ale should be clear and good [683]. This explains the regulation at Coventry in 1421 that ale 'new under the here syve [hair sieve]' was to sell for 1¼d. the gallon, and that 'good and stale' for 1½d. [684] At Seaford there was a third state, 'in the hoffe,' or 'huff,' which sold for 2d [685].

So far were the brewers regarded as the servants of the people that not only was their brewing strictly regulated, but they were compelled to brew even when they considered that new ordinances [686] or a rise in the price of malt would make their trade unprofitable; [687] and in 1434 the brewers of Oxford were summoned to St. Mary's Church and there ordered to provide malt, and to see to it that two or three brewers brewed twice or thrice every week, and sent out their ale [688]. At Gloucester, [689] in the sixteenth century, the brewers were expected to give some kind of weak wort, possibly the scum or dregs of their brew, to the poor to make up into a kind of very small beer, which must have been something like the 'second washing of the tuns,' which formed the perquisite of the under brewers at Rochester Priory [690]. At Norwich barm or yeast was a similar subject of charity, and in 1468 it was set forth that 'wheras berme otherwise clepid goddisgood, without tyme of mynde hath frely be yoven or delyvered for brede whete malte egges or othir honest rewarde to the value only of a farthyng at the uttermost and noon warned (i.e., denied), because it cometh of the grete grace of God; certeyn ... comon brewers ... for ther singler lucre and avayle have nowe newely begonne to take monye for their seid goddisgood,' charging a halfpenny or a penny for the least amount, therefore the brewers were to swear that 'for the time ye or your wife exercise comon brewing ye shall graunte and delyver to any person axyng berme called goddisgood takyng for as moche goddisgood as shall be sufficient for the brewe of a quarter malte a ferthyng at the moost,' provided that they have enough for their own use, and that this do not apply to any 'old custom' between the brewers and bakers [691].

About the end of the fourteenth century a new variety of malt liquor, beer, was introduced from Flanders. It seems to have been imported into Winchelsea as early as 1400, [692] but for the best part of a century its use was mainly, and its manufacture entirely, confined to foreigners. Andrew Borde, [693] who disapproved of it, says, 'Bere is made of malte, of hoppes and water: it is a naturall drynke for a Dutche man. And nowe of late dayes it is moche used in Englande to the detryment of many Englysshe men; specyally it kylleth them the which be troubled with the colycke and the stone and the strangulion; for the drynke is a colde drynke; yet it doth make a man fat, and doth inflate the bely, as it dothe appeare by the Dutche mens faces and belyes. If the bere be well served and be fyned and not new it doth qualify the heat of the lyver.' That, thanks to the large foreign settlement in London, beer brewing soon attained considerable dimensions in the city is evident from the fact that in 1418, when provisions were sent to Henry V. at the siege of Rouen, 300 tuns of 'ber' were sent from London, and only 200 tuns of ale, but the beer was valued at only 13s. 4d. the tun, while the ale was 20s [694]. About the middle of the fifteenth century large quantities of hops were being imported at Rye and Winchelsea, and in the church of the neighbouring village of Playden may still be seen the grave of Cornelius Zoetmann, ornamented with two beer barrels and a crossed mash-stick and fork [695]. A little later we find beer being exported from the Sussex ports and also from Poole, [696] which had long done a large trade in ale to the Channel Islands.

Such beer brewers as occur during the fifteenth century almost all bear foreign names. For instance, in 1473, Thomas Seyntleger and John Goryng of

Southwark recovered heavy damages for theft against John Doys of St. Botolph's-outside-Aldgate and Gerard Sconeburgh of Southwark, 'berebruers,' whose sureties were Godfrey Speryng and Edward Dewysse, also 'berebruers' [697]. Probably in this case the theft was an illegal seizure or distraint of goods for a debt for beer supplied, as although most of the goods said to be stolen were armour and objects of value, such as a book of Gower's poems and an illuminated Sege of Troye, there were also ten barrels of 'sengilbere,' thirty-five barrels of 'dowblebere,' ten lastys of barrels and kilderkins, and two great sacks for 'hoppys.' There was still a prejudice against beer, and in 1471, at Norwich, the use of hops and 'gawle' in brewing was forbidden, [698] while in 1519 the authorities at Shrewsbury prohibited the employment of the 'wicked and pernicious weed, hops' [699]. In the same way, in 1531, the royal brewer was forbidden to use hops or brimstone, but an Act of Parliament passed in the same year bore testimony to the establishment of the industry by exempting alien brewers from the penal statutes against foreigners practising their trades in England, and also by allowing beer brewers to employ two coopers while ale brewers might only employ one [700]. At the same time the barrel of beer was fixed at thirty-six gallons, and that of ale at thirty-two, the kilderkin and firkin being respectively half and quarter of those amounts.

From this time the brewing of beer steadily prospered, the Leakes of Southwark [701] and other alien brewers amassing great riches, English brewers following in their footsteps, and the taste for beer spreading through the country so rapidly that in 1577 Harrison in his Description of England could speak contemptuously of the old ale as thick and fulsome and no longer popular except with a few.

William Harrison, writing about 1577, says: 'In some places of England there is a kind of drinke made of apples, which they call cider or pomage, but that of peares is named pirrie, and both are ground and pressed in presses made for the nonce. Certes, these two are verie common in Sussex, Kent, Worcester, and other steads where these sorts of fruits do abound, howbeit they are not their onelie drinke at all times, but referred unto the delicate sorts of drinke' [702]. A generation earlier Andrew Borde, whom we have already quoted for ale and beer, wrote: 'Cyder is made of the juce of peeres, or of the juce of apples; and other whyle cyder is made of both; but the best cyder is made of cleane peeres, the which be dulcet; but the beste is not praysed in physycke, for cyder is colde of operacyon, and is full of ventosyte, wherfore it doth ingendre evyll humours and doth swage to moche the naturall heate of man and doth let dygestyon and doth hurte the stomacke; but they the whych be used to it, yf it be dronken in harvyst it doth lytell harme.'

Andrew Borde makes no distinction between cider and perry. We find mention of the latter in 1505, when a foreign ship entered Poole with a cargo of apples, pears, etc., and '3 poncheons de pery,' valued at 10s., [703] but references to perry are not numerous. Cider, on the other hand, we find in constant demand from the middle of the twelfth century onwards. It figures on the Pipe Rolls of Henry II., [704] and the contemporary historian and journalist, Gerald de Barri, alleged its use by the monks of Canterbury instead of Kentish ale as an instance of their luxury [705]. A little later, in 1212, the sale of cider is one of the numerous sources of the income of the Abbey of Battle; [706] part of this cider may have come from its estates at Wye, which produced a good deal of cider during the fourteenth century [707].

Possibly the industry was introduced from Normandy, from which district large quantities of cider were imported into Winchelsea about 1270, [708] and this might account for the hold which it took upon Sussex. In the western part of the county, at Pagham, we find mention of an apple mill and press having been wrongfully seized by the escheator's officer in 1275, [709] and at the same place in 1313 the farmer of the archbishop's estates accounted for 12s. spent on buying four casks in which to put cider, on repairing a ciderpress, and on the wages of men hired to make cider [710]. It is, however, in the Nonae Rolls of 1341 that the extent of the cider industry in Sussex is most noticeable [711]. In no fewer than eighty parishes, of which seventy-four were in West Sussex, the tithes of cider are mentioned as part of the endowment of the church, and in another twenty-eight cases the tithes of apples are entered. Moreover the value of these tithes was very considerable, reaching 100s. in Easebourne, and as much as 10 marks (£6, 13s. 4d.) at Wisborough. In the last-named parish in 1385, William Threle granted to John Pakenham and his wife certain gardens and orchards, reserving to himself half the trees bearing fruit either for eating or for cider (mangable et ciserable), in return for which they were to render yearly a pipe of cider and a quarter of store apples (hordapplen); he also retained the right of access to the 'wringehouse,' or building containing the press, and the right to use their ciderpress for his fruit [712].

Beyond an abundance of casual references to cider presses and to the purchases and sale of cider, there is little to record of the industry in medieval times; nor need we devote much attention to the manufacture of wine in England. Domesday Book shows us that the great Norman lords in many cases planted vines near their chief seats, and not many years later William of

Malmesbury spoke of the Vale of Gloucester as planted more thickly with vineyards than any other part of England, and producing the best grapes, from which a wine little inferior to those of France was made. Vines continued to be grown by the great lords and monasteries, but the wine was used entirely for their own consumption, and in decreasing quantities. About 1500 an Italian visitor speaks of having eaten English grapes, and adds 'wine might be made in the southern parts, but it would be harsh,' [713] from which we may judge that such wine making as had existed was at an end by the sixteenth century.

Chapter 11

THE CONTROL OF INDUSTRY

The control of industry is a subject for the treatment of which there are materials sufficient for more than one large volume. I do not, however, regret that I can devote comparatively small space to the subject, as its principles are simple and admit of broad treatment. There is, moreover, in the case of the student who is not a specialist, a danger of obscuring the outlines with a multiplicity of detail. And there is also the danger of selecting some puzzling and obscure incident or enactment, due to local causes of which we are ignorant, and using it as a basis for ingenious generalisations. Broadly speaking, the Control of Industry may be said to be either External, by parliamentary or municipal legislation, or Internal, by means of craft gilds. These two sections again admit of subdivision according as their objects are the protection of the consumer, the employer or the workman. Nor can we entirely ignore legislation for purposes of revenue—subsidies, customs, and octroi dues.

Of industrial legislation by the King's Council, the predecessor of Parliament, we find very little trace. The royal charters of the twelfth century confirming or licensing craft gilds may be more justly regarded as revenue enactments, their object being rather to secure a certain annual return from the craft to which the royal protection was granted than to exercise any control over the craft. The proclamation in the early thirteenth century of the Assize of Cloth and of the Assize of Bread and Ale may be considered to mark the beginning of a national control of industry, though in each case existing regulations were formally adopted rather than new rules imposed. The growth of the towns and the rise of a wealthy merchant class during the reign of Henry III. brought about the birth of Parliament, and naturally led to a certain amount of trade legislation. But with trade—the distribution of finished products by persons other than the producers—we are not concerned. Edward III. , thanks perhaps to his queen Philippa, from the cloth land of Hainault, realised the possibilities of the English cloth manufacture, and endeavoured to foster it by a series of statutes to which reference has been made above. During his reign, in 1349, the Black Death, that great landmark in medieval history, by reducing the numbers of the craftsmen increased the market value of the survivors, who at once demanded and obtained higher wages. Parliament retorted by passing the Statute of Labourers, [714] according to which no smith, carpenter, mason, tiler, shipwright, leather-worker, tailor, or other artificer was to take higher wages than he had received three years earlier, before the pestilence. Though this was legislation in favour of the employer, it was not exactly a case of favouring the wealthy, for by imposing a penalty on the giver of excessive wages as well as upon the receiver, an attempt was made to prevent the small employer being deprived of his workmen by richer rivals. The Act was, so far as we can judge, inspired partly by fear that the capitalist might control the sources of labour, and partly by fear that those sources might get beyond control. Whatever its origin, the statute failed in its expressed intention, and wages remained, as Thorold Rogers has shown, [715] permanently higher. This was not due to any laxity in applying the Act; for many years after it was passed justices were appointed in every part of England to enforce it, [716] but the records of their proceedings, as for instance in Somerset in 1360, [717] where many hundreds of offenders are named, show that the workmen had no hesitation in demanding, and found no difficulty in getting wages higher than the law allowed. Wholesale imprisonment as a remedy for scarcity of labour was scarcely satisfactory, and the small fines which were inflicted proved no deterrent.

As the position of the artificer had improved after the Black Death, so the crafts in general were assuming a greater importance in public estimation, and from about 1380 onwards the regulation of industries occupies an increasing amount of space on the Statute Rolls. With their growing influence, most of the crafts began to make their voices heard crying out for protection, which was usually given them with a liberal hand. But, although the pernicious effects of protective measures (deterioration of quality and rise of price) were to a large extent checked by the control kept over quality and prices by the national and municipal authorities, the consumer was sometimes roused to action. One of the best instances of the struggle between public and private interests is to be found in the case of the Yarmouth herring fishery. Edward III. had granted to Yarmouth the monopoly of the sale of herrings on the east coast during the season of the fishery. As a consequence the price of herrings had risen enormously, and the king was driven to cancel the privilege: the men of Yarmouth at once began to pull the strings, and in 1378 recovered their monopoly, with the same result as before. Once more the consumer made his voice heard, and in 1382 the Yarmouth charter was revoked, only to be restored in 1385 on the ground that without protection of this kind Yarmouth would be ruined.

If a large number of parliamentary enactments were protective of the producer, as for instance the prohibition in 1463 of the import of a vast variety of goods, from silk ribbands to dripping-pans, and from razors to tennis balls, including such incompatibles as playing cards and sacring bells, [718] yet still more were protective of the consumer. For one thing, of course, a single Act prohibiting certain imports might protect a dozen classes of manufactures, while the denunciation of one particular species of fraud would probably lead ingenious swindlers to invent a succession of others, each requiring a separate Act for its suppression. Sentimental admirers of the past are apt to imagine that the medieval workman loved a piece of good work for its own sake and never scamped a job. Nothing could be further from the truth. The medieval craftsman was not called a man of craft for nothing! He had no more conscience than a plumber, and his knowledge of ways that are dark and tricks that are vain was extensive and peculiar. The subtle craft of the London bakers, who, while making up their customer's dough, stole a large portion of the dough under their customers' eyes by means of a little trap-door in the kneading-board and a boy sitting under the counter, [719] was exceptional only in its ingenuity. Cloth was stretched and strained to the utmost and cunningly folded to hide defects, a length of bad cloth would be joined on to a length of superior quality, or a whole cheap cloth substituted for the good cloth which the customers had purchased; inferior leather was faked up to look like the best, and sold at night to the unwary; pots and kettles were made of bad metal which melted when put on the fire; and everything that could be weighed or measured was sold by false measure.

Prior to the middle of the sixteenth century parliamentary attention was mainly concentrated on the cloth trade, and the preambles to the various statutes show that those in authority, including the more responsible manufacturers, realised that honesty is the best policy in the end. In 1390 it was pointed out that the frauds of the west country clothiers had not only endangered the reputations, and even the lives, of merchants who brought them for export, but had brought dishonour on the English name abroad [720]. Two years later it was the reputation of Guildford cloths that had been damaged by sharp practices [721]. The worsteds of Norfolk had early come into favour on the Continent, but in 1410 the Flemish merchants became exasperated at their bad quality, [722] and thirty years later the foreign demand for worsteds had been almost killed, [723] while in 1464 English cloth in general was in grave disrepute, not only abroad, but even in its native land, foreign cloth being largely imported [724]. To give them their due, the gilds recognised the importance to their own interests of maintaining a high standard of workmanship, and co- operated loyally with the municipal authorities to that end.

Although we have classed the control of industries by municipal by-laws as 'external,' and control by gild regulations as 'internal,' no hard and fast line can really be drawn between the two. In England, in contrast to the experience of many Continental states, the two authorities worked together with very little friction, the craft gilds recognising the paramount position of the merchant gild or town council, and the latter, in turn, protecting the interest of the gilds and using their organisation to control the various crafts. The question of the origin of gilds is interesting rather than important, and has given rise to much discussion. It is known that the Roman crafts were organised into collegia, but while it is quite possible that some of the trade gilds in Constantinople, and even in Italy and Spain, might be able to trace their pedigrees back to Roman times, it is more than improbable that there was any connection between the Roman collegia and the English craft gilds of the twelfth century. The gilds of which we find mention in Anglo-Saxon records were clearly fraternities of purely social and religious import. These gilds, friendly societies for the support of religious observances benefiting the souls of all the members, and for the mutual relief of such members as had met with misfortune, survived the Conquest and increased greatly, till by the end of the fourteenth century there could have been hardly a village without at least one gild. It is natural to suppose that in towns, where the choice of gilds was considerable, there would be a tendency for members of the same trade to join the same gild. The strength gained by such union under the common bond of an oath to obey the same statutes and the same officers, and the advantage of the Church's protection must soon have become obvious, and as in 1378 we find the weavers of London forming a fraternity whose ordinances are entirely of a religious nature and contain no reference to the occupation of the members, [725] so we may well believe that many of the early gilds, while apparently purely religious, were in fact trade unions. Whatever may have been the methods in which craft gilds came into existence, we find them increasing in numbers and influence from the middle of the twelfth century onwards.

Meanwhile, however, the capitalists and wealthy traders by means of 'merchant gilds' and similar bodies had so firmly established an oligarchic control over the towns and boroughs that they were able to keep the craft gilds in a subordinate position. Everywhere the town authorities, whether they were mayor and council, or gild merchant, or governors, could impose regulations upon the crafts, while such rules as the crafts drew up for their own management were legal only if accepted by the town council. The case of Coventry was typical, where, in 1421, the mayor and councillors summoned the wardens of the crafts with their ordinances. 'And the poyntes that byn lawfull good and honest for the Cite be alowyd hem and all other thrown asid and had for none' [726]. In the same way at Norwich in 1449, the mayor drew up a complete set of ordinances for the crafts [727]. But although keeping a firm hand on the gilds, and taking measures to protect the interests of the consumers and of the town in general, the civic authorities left the gilds in control of the internal affairs of their crafts. So that the craftsman in his relations to another of the same trade was a gild brother, but in his relations to all other men he was a townsman.

From the consumer's point of view the regulation of prices was perhaps the most important problem. The price of raw material was too dependent upon supply and demand to admit of much regulation, though in 1355 Parliament interfered to bring down the price of iron, [728] forbidding its export, and ordering the Justices of Labourers (i.e., those appointed to enforce the Statute of Labourers) to punish all who sold it too high. The local authorities, civic and manorial, took constant measures to prevent the artificial enhancement of what we may call raw food stuffs, corn, fish, and meat, the 'regrator and forestaller,' that is to say, the middleman, who intercepted supplies before they reached the market and forced prices up for his own sole benefit, being universally regarded as a miscreant [729]. The economists of that period had not grasped the fact that the cleverness shown in buying an article cheap and selling the same thing, without any further expenditure of labour, dear, if done on a sufficiently large scale, justifies the bestowal of the honour of knighthood or a peerage. In the case of manufactured food stuffs, such as bread and ale, the price was automatically fixed by the price of the raw material, and in general prices of manufactures were regulated by the cost of the materials. Even in the case of such artistic work as the making of waxen images, it was considered scandalous that the makers should charge as much as 2s. the pound for images when wax was only 6d. the pound, and in 1432 the waxchandlers were ordered not to charge for workmanship more than 3d. the pound over the current price of wax [730]. The principle that the craftsman should be content with a reasonable profit, and not turn the casual needs of his neighbours to his own benefit is constantly brought out in local regulations, as, for instance, in London in 1362, when in consequence of the damage wrought by a great storm tiles were in great demand, and the tilers were ordered to go on making tiles and selling them at the usual prices [731].

The question of prices, which were thus so largely composed of a varying sum for material, and a fixed sum for workmanship, is very intimately connected with the question of wages [732]. The medieval economist seems to have accepted the Ruskinian theory that all men engaged in a particular branch of trade should be paid equal wages—with the corollary that the better workman would obtain the more employment—as opposed to the modern practice of payment according to skill, which results in the greater employment of the bad workman because he is cheap [733]. There were, of course, grades in each profession, as master or foreman, workman, and assistant or common labourer, but within each grade the rate of payment was fixed—at least within the jurisdiction of any gild or town authority [734] —unless the work was of quite exceptional nature, as, for instance, the making of carved stalls for the royal chapel at Westminster in 1357, where the rates of pay were almost double those of ordinary workmen [735]. Wages were at all times paid on the two systems of piece-work and time, and the hours, which varied in the different trades, and at different places and periods, were as a rule long [736]. For the building trade at Beverley in the fifteenth century work began in summer (from Easter to 15th August) at 4 A.M., and continued till 7 P.M.; at 6 A.M. there was a quarter of an hour's interval for refreshment, at 8 half an hour for breakfast, at 11 an hour and a half to dine and sleep, and at 3 half an hour for further refreshment. During the winter months they worked from dawn till dusk, with half an hour for breakfast at 9 o'clock, an hour for dinner at noon, and a quarter of an hour's interval at 3. These hours agree fairly well with those laid down by Parliament in 1496, [737] which were, from mid-March to mid- September, start at 5 and stop work between 7 and 8, with half an hour for breakfast and an hour and a half for dinner and sleep (the siesta was only to be taken from beginning of May to end of July, during the rest of the time there was to be an hour for dinner and half an hour for lunch—'nonemete'). The blacksmiths of London worked, at the end of the fourteenth century, from dawn till 9 P.M., except during November, December, and January, when their hours were from 6 A.M. to 8 P.M. [738] In the case of the Cappers' gild at Coventry the journeymen's hours were in 1496 from 6 A.M. to 6 P.M.; [739] but in 1520 they had been increased, being from 6 A.M. to 7 P.M. in winter, and from 5 A.M. to 7 P.M. in summer [740]. Wages, of course, when paid by the day, varied in winter and summer, if we may use these terms for the short and long days. In London the determining dates were Easter and Michaelmas, [741] at Bristol Ash Wednesday and St. Calixtus (14th October), [742] and in the case of the workmen at Westminster the Purification (2nd February) and All Saints (1st November), giving an exceptionally short winter period [743].

Against the long hours we have to set the comparative frequency of holidays. On Sundays and all the greater festivals, as well as a variable number of local festivals, such as the dedication day of the Church, no work was done, and on Saturdays and the days preceding festivals work as a rule ceased at four o'clock or earlier. This early closing was enforced at Norwich [744] in 1490, on the representation of the shoemakers that many of their journeymen were 'greatly disposed to riot and idelnes, whereby may succede grete poverte, so that dyuers days wekely when them luste to leve ther bodyly labour till a grete parte of the weke be almost so expended and wasted ... also contrary to the lawe of god and good guydyng temporall they labour quikly toward the Sondaye and festyuall dayes on the Saterdayes and vigils fro iiij of the clock at after none to the depnes and derknes of the nyght foloweng. And not onely that synfull disposicion but moche warse so offendyng in the morownynges of such festes and omyttyng the heryng of the dyvyne servyce.' In the case of the founders in London, [745] while no ordinary metal work, such as turning, filing, or engraving, might be done after noon had rung, an exception had to be made in the case of a casting which was actually in progress; such work might be completed after time, as otherwise the metal would have to be remelted, even if it were not spoilt by the interruption. So far as Sundays and feasts were concerned no work was permitted except in the case of farriers, who were expected to shoe the horses of strangers passing through the town [746]. A good many shops were open on the Sunday morning until seven o'clock, especially shoemakers, [747] who in Bristol were allowed at any time of the day to serve 'eny knyght or Squyer or eny other straunger goyng on her passage or journee, merchant or maryner comyng fro the see,' or, during the six Sundays of harvest, any one else who required boots. [748] Markets during the early part of the thirteenth century were often held on Sundays, but most of these were soon shifted on to week days; and fairs were usually associated with a saint's day, but a fair was an amusement at which the ordinary craftsman was an interested spectator, though the chapmen and merchants were kept busy enough. The London rule that Saturdays and vigils counted for wages as complete days, but that no payment was to be made for the Sundays and feast days [749] was generally observed, but in the case of workmen engaged in building operations at Westminster and the Tower the custom was that wages should be paid for alternate feast days, but not for any Sundays [750].

Rules against working at night or after dark are constantly found in all classes of industries, 'by reason that no man can work so neatly by night as by day' [751]. There was the additional reason that in many trades night work was a source of annoyance to neighbours. This was certainly the case with the blacksmiths, [752] and was probably the cause of the enactment by the Council in 1398, that no leather worker should work by night with hammer and shears, knife or file, at making points or lanyers (laces or thongs). [753] Worst of all these offenders were the spurriers, [754] for 'many of the said trade are wandering about all day without working at all at their trade; and then when they have become drunk and frantic, they take to their work, to the annoyance of the sick and all their neighbourhood .... And then they blow up their fires so vigorously that their forges begin all at once to blaze, to the great peril of themselves and of all the neighbourhood round.' Nuisances of this nature the authorities put down by stringent by-laws, in the same way that they banished offensive occupations, such as the flaying of carcases, the dressing of skins, and the burning of bricks, outside the walls [755].

A third reason for the prohibition of night work was that candlelight not only made good work more difficult, but made bad work more easy. Not only was it easy to pass off faked leather and other deceitful goods by the uncertain, artificial light, which was one of the causes that moved the Council to try to put down 'evechepyngs,' [756] or evening markets, in London, but it also enabled fraudulent workmen to avoid the eye of the vigilant searcher or inspector [757]. All such evasion and secrecy was rightly regarded as suspicious, and at Bristol, to take a single instance, weavers had to work at looms visible from the public street, and not in cellars or upstair rooms, [758] the better class of furs had also to be worked in public, [759] and ale might not be sold in private [760]. The medieval system of search or inspection was very thorough, in theory and, so far as we can judge, in practice also. The search of weights and measures, provisions, cloth, and tanned leather usually belonged to the mayor or equivalent borough officer, or in country districts to the manorial lord, but usually with other manufactures, and very often in the case of cloth and leather, the mayor deputed the duty of search to members of the craft gilds elected and sworn for that purpose. They could inspect the wares either in the workshops, or when exposed for sale, and seize any badly made articles. The forfeited goods were either burnt or given to the poor, [761] and the offending craftsman fined, set in the pillory, or, if an old offender, banished from the town [762]. To facilitate tracing the responsibility for bad work, weavers, fullers, hatters, metal workers, tile-makers, and other craftsmen, including bakers, were ordered to put their private trademarks on their wares [763].

The process of search must have been much simplified by the custom so prevalent in medieval towns of segregating or localising the trades, [764] so that all the goldsmiths dwelt in one quarter, the shoemakers in another, the clothiers in a third, and so forth. How far this was compulsory, and how far a mere matter of custom it is hard to say, but for those who in addition to or instead of shops sold by barrows or chapmen, definite districts were usually assigned. So the London shoemakers might only send out their goods to be hawked between Sopers Lane and the Conduit, and then only in the morning, [765] and at Bristol smiths were not to send ironware through the town for sale in secret places, but either to sell 'in here howse opynlych' or else at their assigned place by the High Cross, where also all strangers coming with 'eny penyworthes yclepid smyth ware' were to stand [766]. The principle of segregation was carried out still more strictly, as we might expect, in the markets. A list of the stalls in the provision market at Norwich in 1397 [767] shows forty butchers' stalls together, followed by forty-five fishmongers and twenty-eight stalls in the poulterers' market, of which nine were used for fresh fish; then there were fifteen shops belonging to the corporation in the wool-market, and the great building of the 'Worthsted Celd,' to which all worsteds sent in from the country had to be brought [768]. Other trades were localised in the same way, and the two divisions of leather-workers, the cordwainers and the workers of the inferior 'bazan' or sheep's leather, were bidden each to keep to their own set of stalls to prevent confusion and fraud [769].

As the trades were kept each to its own district, so was the craftsman restricted to his own trade. By a law issued in 1364 artificers were obliged to keep to one 'mystery' or craft, [770] an exception being made in favour of women acting as brewers, bakers, carders, spinners, and workers of wool and linen and silk,—the versatility of woman, the 'eternal amateur,' being thus recognised some five centuries and a half before Mr. Chesterton rediscovered it. Later statutes forbade shoemakers, tanners, and curriers to infringe on each other's province. It is true that at Bristol [771] we find a puzzling regulation that if a man who had not been apprenticed to tanning practises the craft to which he was apprenticed and also uses the craft of tanning, he shall not pay anything to the tanner's craft but to his own craft and his 'maistier servaunt de tanneres-crafte' shall discharge the dues, etc., of a master of the craft. But probably this belongs to the later fifteenth century after the rise of capitalist employers; if not, it is certainly exceptional, the general tendency being to keep trades, and more especially the allied trades, separate, in order presumably to avoid the growth of 'combines' and monopolies. For this reason fishmongers and fishermen were forbidden to enter into partnership in London, [772] because the dealers, knowing the needs of the city, would be able to manipulate supplies and keep up prices. The case against allowing all the branches of one trade to come under single control is vividly set out in the case of the Coventry iron workers in 1435: [773] — 'Be hit known to you that but yif certen ordenaunses of Craftes withein this Cite, and in speciall the craft of wirdrawerz, be takon good hede to, hit is like myche of the kynges pepull and in speciall poor chapmen and Clothemakers in tyme comeng shallon be gretely hyndered; and as hit may be supposed the principall cause is like to be amonges hem that han all the Craft in her own hondes, That is to say, smythiers, brakemen, [774] gurdelmen and cardwirdrawers; for he that hathe all these Craftes may, offendyng his consience, do myche harme. First in the smethyng, yif he be necligent and mysrule his Iron that he wirkithe be onkynd hetes or elles in oder maner, the whiche when hit is so spilt is not to make no maner chapmannes ware of, Neverthelater for his own eese he will com to his Brakemon and sey to hym:—"Here is a ston of rough-iron the whiche must be tendurly cherysshet." And then the Brakemon most nedes do his maisters comaundement and dothe all that is in hym; and then when the Brakemon hathe don his occupacion, that that the mayster supposithe wilnot in no wyse be holpen atte gurdell, then hit shall be solde for hoke wire.

And when hit is made in hokes and shulde serve the Fisher to take fisshe, when comythe hit to distresse, then for febulness hit all-to brekithe and thus is the Fissher foule disseyved to hys grete harme. And then that wire that the mayster supposithe will be cherisshed atte gurdell, he shall com to his girdelmon and sey to him as he seid to the brakemon:—"Lo, here is a stryng or ij that hathe ben mysgoverned atte herthe; my brakemon hathe don his dener, I prey the do now thyne." And so he dothe as his maister biddethe hyme. And then he gothe to his cardwirdrawer and seithe the same to hym, and he dothe as his maister biddithe hym. And then when the Cardmaker hathe bought this wire thus dissayvabely wrought he may not know hit tille hit com to the crokyng, [775] and then hit crachithe and farithe foule; so the cardmaker is right hevy therof but neverthelater he sethe because hit is cutte he must nedes helpe hymself in eschuing his losse, he makithe cardes therof as well as he may. And when the cardes ben solde to the clothemaker and shuldon be ocupied, anon the teeth brekon and fallon out, so the clothemaker is foule disseyved. Wherfore, sirs, atte reverens of God in fortheryng of the kynges true lege peapull and in eschueng of all disseytes, weithe this mater wysely and ther as ye see disseyte is like to be, therto settithe remedy be your wyse discressions. For ye may right welle know be experience that and the smythier and the brakemen wern togider, and no mo, and the cardwirdrawers and the middlemen [776] togider, and no mo, then hit were to suppose that ther shuld not so myche disseyvaball wire be wrought and sold as ther is; for and the craft were severed in the maner as hit is seide above, then the cardwirdrawers and the myddelmen most nedes bye the wire that they shull wirche of the smythier, and yif the cardwirdrawer were ones or thies disseyved with ontrewe wire he wolde be warre and then wold he sey unto the smythier that he bought that wire of:—"Sir, I hadde of you late badde wire. Sir, amend your honde, or, in feith, I will no more bye of you." And then the smythier, lest he lost his custumers, wolde make true goode; and then, withe the grase of Godd, the Craft shulde amend and the kynges peapull be not disseyved with ontrewe goode.'

The interests of the craftsmen, or producers, were as a whole opposed to those of the consumers. It is true that they co-operated, as we have seen, with the local authorities in maintaining the standard of workmanship, because the craft that did not do so would soon find itself 'defamed and out of employ,' [777] but it was obviously to their interest to keep up prices by the limitation of competition and of output. Their success in restricting competition varied very greatly in different trades and places. In Lincoln, for instance, no tiler might come to work in the town without joining the tilers' gild, [778] while in Worcester, so far was this from being the case, that the tilers were not even allowed to form a gild at all [779]. As a whole the gilds had the townsmen behind them in their opposition to outsiders. The traditional attitude of the Englishman towards a stranger has always been to 'heave half a brick at him,' and as far back as 1421 the authorities at Coventry had to order 'that no man throw ne cast at noo straunge man, ne skorn hym' [780]. The sense of civic, or even parochial, patriotism was more developed in those times, and it was generally felt that while artificers ought not to work for outsiders unless there was no work to be had within the town, on the other hand, employers ought to give the preference to their fellow townsmen and not send work out of the town [781]. As to encouraging strangers to settle within their walls, sentiment varied in different places. At Beverley in 1467 it was enacted that any person might come and set up in his craft without any payment for the first year—except a contribution towards the church light and the yearly pageant maintained by his craft—but after that he should pay yearly 12d. to the town and 12d. to his craft until he became a burgess and member of the gild [782].

But the attitude of Bristol, where no one might weave unless he became a burgess (and a gild brother) was more typical of the general feeling [783]. There was, however, at Bristol a rule that a stranger who had come to the town on a visit, or to wait for a ship might work at his trade for his support during his stay [784]. This rule did not hold good, apparently, at Hereford, as a London tailor, whose master had allowed him during an outbreak of plague to go and stay with relations in Hereford, was imprisoned by the wardens of the local tailors' gild because he did some tailoring for the cousin with whom he was staying, in order to pay for his keep [785]. At Norwich, by the ordinances of 1449, no 'foreign dweller' might have any apprentices or even a hired servant unless the latter was absolutely necessary for his business, and in that case at the end of a year he must either 'buy himself a freeman,' or, if too poor to buy the franchise, 'live under tribute to the sheriffs' [786].

One advantage that the resident manufacturer had over the foreigner was that his wares entered the local market without the handicap of paying customs or octroi dues. Long lists of these dues on every conceivable kind of merchandise, from bears and monkeys to peppercorns, are to be found in the records of many towns, [787] more especially seaports. It is true that the burgesses of many towns, and the tenants of many religious houses were theoretically exempt from paying these dues, but it is probable that the delay and worry of proving such exemption was often felt to be a greater loss than payment. So far as the alien importer was concerned, although there was no such thing as a protective duty (the import of an article was either prohibited altogether or unrestrained), he might find himself called upon to pay a higher, even a double, import duty on all his merchandise. This policy of discriminating against the alien, combined with the continual harassing of the unfortunate foreign merchants, induced many alien settlers to take out letters of naturalisation, and the long lists of these in the fifteenth century [788] show how numerous and widespread these aliens were. Coming for the most part from Flanders and the Low Countries, they settled not only in London and the other great towns, but in the smaller market towns and villages throughout the country, exercising their various trades as goldsmiths, clothmakers, leather-workers, and so forth. In London in particular the foreign element was very large from an early date and, as a result of the invitation issued by Edward III. to foreign clothworkers and their exemption from the control of the native clothiers' gild, we have the exceptional occurrence of a gild of alien weavers. This gild, itself divided by the rivalries and quarrels of the Flemings and Brabanters, [789] was unpopular with the native weavers because, while competing with them for trade, they did not share in the farm or rent paid by the native gild to the king, and in general there was a strong feeling against the aliens in London, which was fanned by the craft gilds and occasionally culminated in rioting, the murder of some of the foreigners and the plunder of their shops.

While the gilds were constantly coming into conflict with outside interests, there was also an internal conflict of interests between the masters, the hired servants, or journeymen, and the intermediate class of apprentices. This becomes more noticeable towards the end of our period.

While there was occasional friction between employer and employed even before the second half of the fourteenth century, it was during the next two centuries that the rise of the capitalist, coupled with the descent of the small independent masters into the position of journeymen, brought about strained relations between the two classes. In the earlier period in most of the trades there was reasonable prospect for any craftsman that he would be able to set up as an independent master, but as time went on the difficulty of attaining independence increased. The growing attraction of town and craft life as compared with agriculture swelled the ranks of the craftsmen, and the gilds, whose management was in the hands of the masters, endeavoured to limit competition by raising their entrance fees and more especially by raising their 'upsets,' that is to say the fees which had to be paid by a craftsman upon setting up as a master. One of the earliest instances of this restriction of competition occurred in connection with the weavers' gild of London, concerning whom it was reported in 1321 that they had during the last thirty years reduced the number of looms in the city from 380 to 80 [790]. In this case the object was to benefit all the members of the gild at the expense of the public, and not to protect existing masters from rivals within the gild, and the method employed was therefore the raising of the fee for entrance to the gild. This same weavers' gild was so far ahead of its times that it had instituted the modern trade unions' restriction of output, no member being allowed to weave a cloth in less than four days, though such a cloth could easily be woven in three if not in two days [791]. But this was a most exceptional move, if not absolutely unique.

How far the desire to restrict output was at the bottom of regulations forbidding the employment of more than a strictly limited number of apprentices and journeymen, and how far such prohibitions were inspired by fear of the monopolisation of labour by capitalists it is difficult to say. Probably the dread of the capitalist was the chief incentive for such regulations, which are very numerous; the cobblers of Bristol, for instance, being restricted to a single 'covenaunt hynd,' [792] and the cappers of

Coventry allowed only two apprentices, neither of whom might be replaced if he left with his master's leave before the end of his term of seven years [793]. The same principle of fair play between employers led to the ordaining of heavy penalties for taking away another man's servant, or employing any journeyman who had not fulfilled his engagement with his previous master, and to the strict prohibition of paying more than the fixed maximum wages. As this last provision was sometimes got over by the master's wife giving his servants extra gratuities and gifts, this practice was forbidden at Bristol in 1408, except that the master might at the end of a year give 'a courtesy' of 20d. to his chief servant [794]. As the unfair securing of labour by offering high wages was forbidden, so the use of the cheap labour of women was as a rule regarded with disfavour. The fullers of Lincoln were forbidden to work with any woman who was not the wife or maid of a master, [795] and the 'braelers,' or makers of braces, of London, in 1355, laid down 'that no one shall be so daring as to set any woman to work in his trade, other than his wedded wife or his daughter' [796]. A century later the authorities at Bristol went even further, for finding that the weavers were 'puttyn, occupien and hiren ther wyfes, doughtours and maidens, some to weve in ther owne lombes and some to hire them to wirche with othour persons of the said crafte,' whereby many 'likkely men to do the Kyng service in his warris, ... and sufficiently lorned in the seid crafte ... gothe vagraunt and unoccupied,' absolutely forbade the practice in future, making an exception only in the case of wives already so employed [797]. Of child labour we hear very little, one of the few notices being an order on their behalf made, suitably enough, by Richard Whittington in 1398, that whereas some 'hurers' (makers of fur caps) send their apprentices and journeymen and children of tender age down to the Thames and other exposed places, amid horrible tempests, frosts, and snows, to scour caps, to the very great scandal of the city, this practice is to cease at once [798].

Apprenticeship was from quite early times the chief, and eventually became the only, path to mastership. The ordinances of the London leather-dressers, [799] made in 1347, and those of the pewterers, [800] made the next year, give as alternative qualifications for reception into the craft the completion of a period of apprenticeship, or the production of good testimony that the applicant is a competent workman. A similar certificate of ability was required of the dyers at Bristol, [801] in 1407, even if they were apprentices, but as a rule the completion of a term of apprenticeship was a sufficient qualification. That term might vary considerably, but the custom of London, which held good in most English boroughs, eventually fixed it at a minimum of seven years. This would often be exceeded, and we find, for instance, a boy of fourteen apprenticed to a haberdasher in 1462 for the rather exceptional term of twelve years; but in this case the master had undertaken to provide him with two years' schooling, the first year and a half to learn 'grammer,' and the next half year to learn to write [802]. In a list of apprentices who took the oath of fealty to the king and the city at Coventry in 1494, the terms range from five to nine years, though the majority were for seven years; during the first years of their terms, they were to receive nominal wages, usually 12d. a year, and for their last year more substantial rewards, varying from 6s. 8d. to 25s [803]. The oath to obey the city laws serves as a reminder that the apprentice, not being a full member of the gild, was under the charge of the city authorities to some extent. Indentures of apprenticeship had as a rule to be enrolled by the town clerk, [804] and in London the transfer of an apprentice from one employer to another was not legal unless confirmed by the city chamberlain [805]. Besides having his indentures enrolled, and paying a fee to the craft gild, the apprentices, or rather his friends, had to give a bond for his good behaviour. The rights of the apprentice, on the other hand, were probably always guarded by a right of appeal to the wardens of his craft: this was certainly the case at Coventry in 1520, the masters of the cappers being obliged to go once a year to all the shops of their craft and call the apprentices before them, and if any apprentice complained three times against his master for 'insufficient finding,' they had power to take him away and put him with another master [806]. As a master's interest in his apprentice was transferable to another master, so it was possible for an apprentice to buy up the remainder of his term after he had served a portion. He could not, however, be received into his gild as a master until the whole of his term had expired, [807] and although it would seem that he could set up in business by himself, [808] probably he might not employ workmen, and as a rule he no doubt spent the unexpired portion of his term as a journeyman.

The journeymen, working by the day (journée), either with their masters, or in their own houses, as opposed to the covenant servants, who were hired by the year, [809] and lived in their employer's house, constituted the fluid element in the industrial organisation, and were composed partly of men who had served a full apprenticeship but lacked funds or enterprise to set up independently, and partly of others who had either served only a brief apprenticeship, or had picked up their knowledge of the craft in other ways [810]. Although more or less free to work for what employers they would, practically all gild regulations contained a stringent order against the employment of any journeyman who had broken his contract or left his late master without good reason [811]. In the matter of home work rules varied; the journeymen of the wiredrawers and allied crafts at Coventry in 1435 were allowed to work at home and might not be compelled to come to their masters' houses, [812] but in London, in 1271, the shoemakers were not allowed to give out work, as the journeymen were found to go off with the goods [813]. The vagaries of this class, indeed, caused much heart-searching to their masters. Instead of being content with their holidays, and accepting their twelve hours' working day, they had a pernicious habit of going off on the spree for two or three days, and amusing themselves by playing bowls, 'levyng ther besynes at home that they shuld lyve by'; [814] and the Coventry employers, with that touching regard for widows and orphans (or in this case wives and children) which has always distinguished the English capitalists, forbade them to frequent inns on workdays, 'as it is daylye seen that they whiche be of the pooreste sorte doo sytte all daye in the alehouse drynkynge and playnge at the cardes and tables and spende all that they can gett prodigally upon themselfes to the highe displeasure of God and theyre owne ympovershynge, whereas if it were spente at home in theyre owne houses theyre wiffes and childerne shulde have parte therof' [815]. Not having any voice in the craft gilds the journeymen were continually forming 'yeomen gilds,' 'bacheleries,' and other combinations, which the masters' gilds usually endeavoured to suppress. In 1387 the London journeymen cordwainers formed a fraternity [816] and endeavoured to secure it by obtaining papal protection; nine years later the mayor and aldermen put down a fraternity formed by the yeomen of the saddlers, at the same time ordering the masters to treat their men well in future, [817] and in 1415 the wardens of the tailors complained that their journeymen had combined, living together in companies in particular houses, where they held assemblies, and adopting a livery, whereupon the council, in view of the danger to the peace of the city from such an uncontrolled and irresponsible body, forbade the combination and ordered the journeymen to live under the governance of the wardens of the craft [818]. The fraternity of the yeomen tailors, however, was not so easily suppressed, and is found two years later petitioning for leave to hold its yearly assembly at St. John's, Clerkenwell [819]. In the same way at Coventry, when the journeymen tailors' gild of St. Anne was suppressed in 1420, they simply changed their patron and reappeared as the gild of St. George, against which measures were taken in 1425 [820]. The charges against the yeomen saddlers in 1396 were, that they had so forced wages up that whereas the masters could formerly obtain a workman for from 40s. to 5 marks yearly and his board they had now to pay 10 or 12 marks or even £10, and that also business was dislocated by the bedel coming round and summoning the journeymen to attend a service for the soul of a deceased brother. The clashing of religious observances with business led to an order at Coventry in 1528 that the journeymen dyers should make no assemblies at weddings, brotherhoods, or burials, nor make any 'caves' (i.e., combinations), but use themselves as servants, and as no craft [821]. This was practically an enforcement of an order issued ten years earlier, that no journeymen should form 'caves' without the licence of the mayor and the master of their craft [822]. Such a licence would not as a rule be granted, unless the masters were unusually broadminded, or the journeymen exceptionally strong. There was, however, at Coventry a recognised fraternity of journeymen weavers in 1424; their wardens paid 12d. to the chief master for every brother admitted; each brother gave 4d. towards the cost of the craft pageant, and the chief master contributed towards the journeymen's altar lamp, while both masters and servants held their feasts together [823]. At Bristol also there was a gild of journeymen connected with the shoemakers' craft, sharing with the craft gild in the expenses of church lights and feasts [824].

The success of the London saddlers in forcing wages up is a remarkable tribute to the power of union; and we find that during the fourteenth century the strike was well known, and when a master would not agree with his workmen the other workmen of the craft would come out and cease work until the dispute was settled [825]. This practice was, of course, forbidden, but we may doubt with what success. At the same time the masters were pretty well unanimous in forbidding the employment of a craftsman whose dispute with his master had not been settled. So far as the offence of detaining wages due was concerned, penalties were often laid down in gild ordinances, [826] while in the case of other disputes the matter would be settled by the council or court of the craft [827]. The existence of a craft gild practically implied a court before which disputes between members of the craft or between craftsmen and customers were tried [828]. Such courts were at first directly under the borough authorities, the mayor or his deputies presiding over the weekly courts of the weavers in London in 1300, [829] and although they seem to have attained a greater degree of independence there seems usually to have been a right of appeal to the borough court [830]. It was probably to avoid this that some of the Coventry masters took to impleading craftsmen in spiritual courts, on the ground that they had broken their oaths in not keeping the gild rules [831].

Too much attention must not be given to the quarrelsome side of the gilds, for they were essentially friendly societies for mutual assistance. One of the rules of the London leather- dressers was that if a member should have more work than he could complete, and the work was in danger of being lost the other members should help him [832]. So also, if a mason wished to undertake a contract he got four or six responsible members of the craft to guarantee his ability, and if he did not do the work well they had to complete it [833]. Again, if a farrier undertook the cure of a horse and was afraid that it would die, he might call in the advice of the wardens of his company, but if he was too proud to do so and the horse died, he would be responsible to the owner [834]. The rule of the weavers at Hull, that none should let his apprentice work for another [835] was not an infringement of the principle of mutual aid, but was designed to prevent evasion of the order that none might have more than two apprentices; the fact that a fine was only exacted in the event of the apprentice so working for more than thirteen days actually points to the loan of temporary assistance being allowed. While help was thus given to the craftsman when in full employ, a still more essential feature of the gilds was their grant of assistance to members who had fallen ill or become impoverished through no fault of their own [836]. Nor did their benevolence end with the poor craftsman's death, for they made an allowance to his widow and celebrated Masses for the repose of his soul. The religious element in the organisation of gilds, though very strong, does not affect us very much in considering their industrial side, but there is one indirect effect which must be referred to. The custom of all the gilds and fraternities going in procession to the chief church of their town on certain feast days, carrying their banners and symbols, gradually developed during the fifteenth century until each gild endeavoured to outshine its rivals in pageantry. Payments towards the pageants were exacted from all members of the trade even if they were not members of the gild, but in spite of this the expenses were so great that the smaller gilds were almost ruined, and consequently we find during the latter half of the fifteenth century schemes to amalgamate, or at any rate to unite for the support of a common pageant, many of the smaller mysteries or crafts. An account of a pageant at Norwich [837] about 1450 is interesting as showing the numbers of these lesser crafts, and the way in which they were combined. Twelve pageants were presented: (1) The Creation of the World, by the mercers, drapers, and haberdashers. (2) Paradise, by the grocers and raffemen. (3) 'Helle Carte,' by the glaziers, stainers, scriveners, parchemyners, the carpenters, gravers, colermakers, and wheelwrights. (4) Abel and Cain, by the shearmen, fullers, 'thikwollenwevers,' and coverlet makers, the masons and limeburners. (5) 'Noyse shipp' (Noah's Ark), by the bakers, brewers, innkeepers, cooks, millers, vintners, and coopers. (6) Abraham and Isaac, by the tailors, broderers, the reders and tylers. (7) Moses and Aaron with the children of Israel and Pharaoh and his knights, by the tanners, curriers, and cordwainers. (8) David and Goliath, by the smiths. (9) The Birth of Christ, by the dyers, calenders, the goldsmiths, goldbeaters, saddlers, pewterers, and braziers. (10) The Baptism of Christ, by the barbers, waxchandlers, surgeons, physicians, the hardwaremen, the hatters, cappers, skinners, glovers, pinners, pointmakers, girdlers, pursers, bagmakers, 'sceppers,' [838] the wiredrawers and cardmakers. (11) The Resurrection, by the butchers, fishmongers, and watermen. (12) The Holy Ghost, by the worsted weavers.

In some cases the smaller crafts seem to have been absorbed into the larger, but in the Norwich regulations of 1449, [839] when general orders were given for the annexation of the smaller crafts to the larger, the bladesmiths, locksmiths, and lorimers, for instance, being united to the smiths, it was laid down that such of the annexed misteries as had seven or more members should elect their own wardens, and that the mayor should appoint wardens for such as had fewer than seven members. This, which is interesting as showing how small some of these misteries were, points to a retention of control, the amalgamation being mainly concerned, no doubt, with the expenses of the pageant and the gild feasts. These latter became so elaborate and costly that many of the unfortunate members chosen as 'feast-makers' were ruined, and in 1495 orders were given at Norwich that the wardens alone should be feast-makers, and that they should provide one supper and one dinner, on the same day, and no more, and that should be at the common expense of the gild [840]. These orders had to be repeated in 1531, and it is rather interesting to read that in 1547 [841] the dishes which had to be provided by the cordwainers' feast-makers were 'frumenty, goos, vell, custard, pig, lamb, and tarte. At soper—colde sute, [842] hot sute, moten, douset, [843] and tarte.'

With the pleasant picture of our craftsman resting from his labours and regaling himself in true English fashion, we may take leave of him and his work.

References

[1] Galloway, Annals of Coal Mining, 5.
[2] See Wright's Uriconium.
[3] Petrie and Sharp, Mon. Hist., i, x.
[4] Printed by the Surtees Society and, more recently, in V. C. H. Durham.
[5] V. C. H. Durham, ii. 293.
[6] Op. cit. (Rolls Ser.), 160.
[7] Galloway, op. cit., 18.
[8] Riley, Mems. of London, p. xvi.
[9] Galloway, op. cit., 30.
[10] Assize R., 223, m. 4.
[11] Mat. Paris, Chron. (Rolls Ser.), vi. 96.
[12] V. C. H. Glouc., ii. 218.
[13] Pat., 40 Hen. III. m. 21.
[14] V. C. H. Shrops. , i. 449.
[15] V. C. H. Derby, ii. 349.
[16] Ann. Mon. (Rolls Ser.), iii. 105.
[17] Pat., 35 Edw. I., m. 5d. Complaints had been made and commissions of inquiry appointed in 1285 (Pat., 13 Edw. I., m. 18d) and 1288 (Pat., 16 Edw. I., m. 12).
[18] Galloway, op. cit., 23.
[19] Colman, Hist. of Barwick in Elmet, 205.
[20] Mins. Accts., bdle. 1040, no. 18.
[21] Journ. Brit. Arch. Ass. , xxix. 174.
[22] Proc. Soc. of Ant., xx. 262.
[23] V. C. H. Lancs., ii. 359.
[24] V. C. H. Derby, ii. 350.

[25] Add. Ch., 49516.
[26] V. C. H. Derby, ii. 351.
[27] Ibid.
[28] V. C. H. Derby, ii. 350.
[29] Ibid., 351. Cf. a reference to 'le dampe' in 1316: Hist. MSS. Com. Rep., Middleton MSS., 88. This Report contains a great deal of value for the early history of coal mining.
[30] V. C. H. Derby, ii. 350.
[31] A 'sowe' is mentioned at Cossall in 1316.— Hist. MSS. Com. Rep., Middleton MSS., 88.
[32] Galloway, op. cit., 53.
[33] Ibid., 46.
[34] Finchale Priory (Surt. Soc.), p. cccxci.
[35] V. C. H. Durham, ii. 322.
[36] V. C. H. War., ii. 221.
[37] In 1366 in the manor of Bolsover, £4, 11s. was paid in wages to 'a man looking after the coals and mine at Shutehoode, and keeping tally against the colliers and diggers of the same coals and stones.'—Foreign R., 42 Edw. III. , m. 13.
[38] Except that the coalminers in the Forest of Dean, thanks to their intimate association with the iron-miners there, shared in the latter's privileges.
[39] V. C. H. Durham, ii. 322.
[40] Exch. Dep. by Com., 29 Eliz., East. 4.
[41] V. C. H. Derby, ii. 352.
[42] 'Fines for digging coals in the lord's waste,' in fifteenth century.— Galloway, op. cit. 76; 'Licences to dig in sixteenth century,' ibid., 113.
[43] Exch. Dep. by Com., 21 Eliz., Hil. 8.
[44] See, e.g., V. C. H. War. , ii. 219; V. C. H. Derby, ii. 350; De Banco R., 275, m. 163d.
[45] Star Chamber Proc., Hen. VIII., file 22, no. 94.
[46] Star Chamber Proc., Edw. VI. , file 6, no. 99.
[47] Rot. Parl., i. 228, 229.
[48] See V. C. H. War. , ii. 219.
[49] The rent was sometimes paid, partly or wholly, in kind; as at Shippen in 1262 (Colman, Hist. of Barwick-in-Elmet, 205).
[50] V. C. H. Shrops. , ii. 454.
[51] V. C. H. Derby, ii. 350.
[52] Such partnerships were not uncommon; e.g., in 1351 W. de Allesworth demanded 2s. 10½d. from Geoffrey Hardyng, as the seventh part of 20s.

paid to Geoffrey and his partners for coal got at Nuneaton.—Add. Ch. 49532.

[53] Galloway, op. cit., 70.

[54] Add. Ch. 48948.

[55] Galloway (op. cit., 113-14) gives a late sixteenth-century case in Wakefield, where the 'heads, pillars, and other works ... for bearing up the ground' being cut away, the ground suddenly fell in.

[56] Galloway, op. cit., 45.

[57] V. C. H. Durham, ii. 324.

[58] Foreign R., 42 Edw. III. , m. E.

[59] Pat., 8 Rich. II.

[60] Rot. Parl., iv. 148.

[61] Galloway, op. cit., 70, 87.

[62] Customs Accts., 106/1.

[63] Ibid., 111/40.

[64] Ibid., 171/26.

[65] Kendall, Iron Ores, 15; V. C. H. Sussex, ii. 241.

[66] Journ. of Brit. Arch. Ass. , xxix. 121-9.

[67] V. C. H. Somers., i. 275. There was also a 'collegium fabrorum' at Chichester (Regnum).— Suss. Arch. Coll., vii. 61-3.

[68] Kemble, Cod. Dipl., no. 30.

[69] Chron. Evesham (Rolls Ser.), 26. The legend was probably invented as an explanation of the remains of the (Roman) town found below the ground here, but the tradition of the smiths had no doubt some foundation.

[70] Dom. Bk., i. 162.

[71] Ibid.

[72] V. C. H. Cumberland, ii. 340.

[73] Facsimiles of Charters in B. M., no. 64.

[74] V. C. H. Derby, ii. 356.

[75] Pipe Rolls, quoted in V. C. H. Gloucs. , ii. 216.

[76] V. C. H. Gloucs. , ii. 217.

[77] V. C. H. Sussex, ii. 241.

[78] See Exch. K. R. Accts., 467, 7.

[79] Ibid., 467, 7 (7).

[80] Ibid., 467, 7 (7).

[81] Roy. and Hist. Letters (Rolls Ser.), i. 278.

[82] Furness Coucher (Chetham Soc.), pt. iii., Intro.

[83] Ibid.

[84] Holinshed, Chron., sub anno.

[85] V. C. H. Derby, ii. 357.

[86] Peat was mixed with the charcoal in Lancashire, and doubtless elsewhere, when available.— V. C. H. Lancs. , ii. 361.

[87] This process was used by the Romans at Beaufort, near Battle, in Sussex, amongst other places.— Suss. Arch. Coll., xxix. 173.

[88] Journ. of Brit. Arch. Ass. , xxix. 124.

[89] Even after the introduction of the footblast the 'cinders' or slag, contained about half the original iron, according to Dud Dudley (Metallum Martis), and were worth resmelting in the improved furnaces of later times.

[90] Engl. Hist. Rev., xiv. 513.

[91] V. C. H. Derby, ii. 358.

[92] Furness Coucher (Chetham Soc.), pt. iii., Intro., and pp. 261-6.

[93] See above, p. 7.

[94] The same term is used in connection with burning tiles, and is no doubt derived from the same root as anneal.

[95] This account of the process of manufacture is compiled from several sources, the chief being: (1) the accounts of Tudeley Forge, Tunbridge, for the reign of Edw. III. , in the P. R. O.; (2) the accounts of Bedbourne Forge, Durham, in 1408, Engl. Hist. Rev., xiv. 509-29; (3) several Sussex accounts summarised by the present writer in V. C. H. Sussex, ii. 244-5.

[96] Nicholls, Iron Making in the Forest of Dean, 20.

[97] Cal. Chart. R., iii. 95-6.

[98] V. C. H. Glouc. , ii. 219, n. 5. Cf. the twelfth century grant to the monks of Louth Park of 'duas fabricas, id est duos focos ... scilicet unam fabricam blomeriam ... unam operariam.'— V. C. H. Derby, ii. 356.

[99] The date of the introduction of hammers driven by water power is problematic: a 'great waterhamor' was working in Ashdown Forest, Sussex, in 1496.—Misc. Bks. Exch. T. R., 8, f. 49.

[100] The unworked bloom was called a 'loop,' which appears to be derived from the French loup, a wolf, the German equivalent, Stück, being applied to such a mass of iron.—Swank, Iron in All Ages, 80.

[101] A furnace once lit might be kept in blast sometimes for as long as forty weeks, in the seventeenth century, but the periods usual in earlier times were no doubt much shorter.

[102] Engl. Hist. Rev., xiv. 529.

[103] Furness Coucher, pt. iii., Intro. The word used is 'band,' but it is apparently equivalent to 'bloom.'
[104] Exch. K. R. Accts., 485, no. 11.
[105] Ibid., 466, no. 20.
[106] Suss. Arch. Coll., ii. 202.
[107] Exch. K. R. Accts., 546, no. 16.
[108] V. C. H. Sussex, ii. 246.
[109] Exch. K. R. Accts., 483, no. 19.
[110] V. C. H. Sussex, ii. 245.
[111] Engl. Hist. Rev., xiv. 509-29.
[112] Exch. K. R. Accts., 485, no. 11.
[113] Mins. Accts., 890, no. 25.
[114] Latinised in one place as 'anteriores flatores.'
[115] Suss. Arch. Coll., xiii. 128.
[116] At some iron mills near Teddesley in Staffordshire in 1583 the filler and fyner were identical, and there was a hammerman and a founder.—Exch. K. R. Accts., 546, no. 16.
[117] Nicholls, Ironmaking in the Forest of Dean; V. C. H. Gloucs. , ii. 219-23.
[118] This was farmed in 1280 for £23, so that the amount exported annually must have been well over 10,000 loads.
[119] The surface material which has to be removed before the ore is reached.
[120] Arch. Cambr. (S. 3), iii. 418.
[121] V. C. H. Sussex, ii. 247
[122] Exch. Dep. by Com., 22 Eliz., Trin. 4.
[123] Journ. Brit. Arch. Ass. , xxxi. 129-42. For a list of Roman pigs found in England, see ibid., liv. 272.
[124] Ibid.
[125] Birch, Cart. Sax., i. 579.
[126] V. C. H. Glouc. , ii. 237.
[127] V. C. H. Derby, ii. 323.
[128] Pipe Rolls of Hen. II.
[129] V. C. H. Durham, ii. 348.
[130] V. C. H. Somers. , ii. 363.
[131] Pat., 20 Hen. III., m. 13.
[132] V. C. H. Cumberland, ii. 339.
[133] V. C. H. Derby, ii. 326.
[134] V. C. H. Somers. , ii. 367-9.
[135] V. C. H. Cumb. , ii. 340.

[136] Pat., 15 Edw. IV., pt. i., m. 22.

[137] Assize R., 143, m. 1. The Scottish king's dominial rights over Alston, apart from the mines, seem to have been well established. William the Lion granted land at Alston as 'in Tyndale,' to William de Vipont, and later to his son Ivo de Vipont, the latter grant being confirmed by King John in 1210. Finally, after the whole matter had been carefully examined, Edward I. gave the manor of Alston in 1282 to Nicholas de Vipont to hold of the King of Scotland, reserving, however, the liberty of the mines.—Assize Rolls, 143, m. 1; 132, m. 34; Chanc. Misc. 53, file 1, nos. 20, 22.

[138] V. C. H. Cumb. , ii. 340.

[139] Assize R., 143, m. 1.

[140] Assize R., 132, m. 34; 143, m. 1.

[141] V. C. H. Derby, ii. 339.

[142] Exch. K. R. Accts., 260, no. 19.

[143] e.g., at Eyam and Litton.— V. C. H. Derby , ii. 338.

[144] Until the nineteenth century the would-be miner had to set up a model stow, fastened with wooden pins and not with nails.

[145] i.e., forwards and backwards along the line of the vein.

[146] It is not quite clear whether he threw from the old pit, in which case he would naturally throw a very short distance, or from his own pit, in which case he might so throw as to cover much of the vein which would have belonged to the elder pitchers.

[147] V. C. H. Derby, ii. 328.

[148] The Derbyshire standard dish made in 1512 and still preserved at Wirksworth contains about sixty lbs. of ore.

[149] Assize R., 132, m. 34.

[150] Ibid.

[151] Memo. R., K. R., Mich., 2 Edw. II. , no. 55.

[152] V. C. H. Derby, ii. 332.

[153] Memo. R., L. T. R., 25-26 Edw. I., m. 51.

[154] The load, or lade (lada), contained nine dishes (disci, scutella).

[155] Exch. K. R. Accts., 260, no. 19.

[156] Ibid., 261, no. 25.

[157] Memo. R., L. T. R., 25-26 Edw. I., m. 51.

[158] In 1302 there were four mines: the South Mine, the Middle Mine, the Mine of Fershull, and the Old Mine.—Exch. K. R. Accts., 260, no. 22.

[159] The smiths were paid 12d.-18d. a week.— Ibid.

[160] Exch. K. R. Accts., 261, no. 25.

[161] Anct. Corresp., xlviii. 81.
[162] Exch. K. R. Accts., 260, no. 16.
[163] Anct. Corresp., xlviii, 81.
[164] Exch. K. R. Accts., 260, no. 22.
[165] Pipe R., 28 Edw. I.
[166] V. C. H. Durham, ii. 349.
[167] Pipe R., 28 Edw. I.
[168] Exch. K. R. Accts., 260, no. 6.
[169] Pipe R., 28 Edw. I.
[170] V. C. H. Somers. , ii. 373.
[171] Exch. K. R. Accts., 260, no. 22.
[172] Archaeologia, lvij, 113-124.
[173] e.g., 'In 6510 turbis tannitis emptis ad inde faciendos cineres pro plumbo affinando.'—Exch. K. R. Accts., 260, no. 4.
[174] Memo., L. T. R., 25-26 Edw. I. , m. 51.
[175] Exch. K. R. Accts., 260, no. 7.
[176] Ibid., no. 19.
[177] Pipe R., 28 Edw. I.
[178] V. C. H. Derby, ii. 324.
[179] It is possible that 'cut' is the Celtic word 'cwt ', meaning a piece, and dates back to British times.— Ibid.
[180] Ibid.
[181] Pipe R., 28 Edw. I.
[182] Pat., 27 Edw. I., m. 28.
[183] Exch. K. R. Accts., 126, no. 9.
[184] Pat., 35 Edw. I., m. 19.
[185] Mins. Accts., 826, no. 12.
[186] Ibid., no. 11.
[187] Exch. K. R. Accts., 265, no. 9.
[188] Ibid. , no. 10.
[189] Close 24 Edw. I., m. 11d.
[190] Pipe R., 28 Edw. I.
[191] Ibid.
[192] Anct. Corresp., xlviii. 177.
[193] 'Minera' may also bear the sense of 'ore.'
[194] Close 7 Edw. II. , m. 6.
[195] Anct. Pet., 13552.
[196] Pat., 17 Edw. II. , p. 2, m. 15.
[197] Assize R., 135, m. 26d.

[198] Pat., 14 Edw. IV., p. 1, m. 7d.
[199] Pat., 15 Edw. IV., p. 1, m. 22.
[200] Pat., 18 Edw. IV. , p. 2, m. 30.
[201] Pat., 2 Edw. IV. , p. 1, m. 7.
[202] Exch. K. R. Accts., 262, no. 2.
[203] Acts of Privy Council, 1542-7, p. 367.
[204] Jour. of Brit. Arch. Ass. , lxii. 145-60.
[205] Archaeologia, lix. 281-8.
[206] V. C. H. Cornw., i. 523.
[207] Ibid.
[208] Vol. iii. of Harvard Economic Studies . The same writer has contributed a valuable article on tin-mining to V. C. H. Cornwall.
[209] Lewis, op. cit., 5.
[210] Lewis, op. cit., 11.
[211] A case of a London goldsmith making engines and instruments to drain a deep tin mine near Truro occurs in first quarter of the sixteenth century—Early Chanc. Proc., 481, no. 46.
[212] Memo. R., L. T. R., 9 Eliz., Mich., 3.
[213] Either the channel by which the blast was admitted, or else the channel conveying water to the wheel.
[214] The ore was sometimes roasted before smelting.
[215] V. C. H. Cornw. , i. 539.
[216] Lewis, op. cit., 133-4.
[217] W. de Wrotham, when appointed warden of the stannaries in 1198, ordered all masters of ships in Cornwall and Devon to swear not to take unstamped tin out of the country.—Lewis, op. cit. , 337.
[218] Lewis, op. cit., 190.
[219] Op. cit., 187.
[220] V. C. H. Cornw. , i. 523.
[221] Lewis, op. cit., 34.
[222] For output, see Lewis, op. cit., App. J.
[223] Lewis, op. cit., App. K.
[224] Ibid., Apps. L-T.
[225] Chron. of Battle Abbey, 11.
[226] V. C. H. Northants. , ii. 293-5.
[227] Ibid., 295.
[228] Fabric R. of York (Surtees Soc.), passim.
[229] e.g., at the Tower in 1324 'one boatload of Aylesford stone called rag, 6s.'—Exch. K. R. Accts., 469, no. 7. And in 1362 '8 boatloads of stone

called ragg, with carriage from Maidstone, £10, 13s. 4d.'— Ibid., 472, no. 9.

[230] Ibid., 502, no. 10.

[231] See the Westminster building accounts, passim.

[232] Arch. Cant., ii. 112.

[233] '20 tontightes de peers de Beer.'—Exch. K. R. Accts., 472, no. 8.

[234] Exch. K. R. Accts., 491, no. 13.

[235] For some fourteenth and fifteenth century references to the Haslebury quarries, see The Tropenell Cartulary (Wilts. Arch. Soc.), ii. 148-50.

[236] V. C. H. Dorset, ii. 333.

[237] Ibid., 339.

[238] V. C. H. Sussex, ii. 230.

[239] Exch. K. R. Accts., 305, no. 12.

[240] Ibid., 502, no. 3.

[241] Arch. Cant., ii. 112.

[242] The 'pondus dolii,' anglicised in other entries as 'tuntight,' seems to have been about 40 cubic feet.

[243] Presumably from the Yorkshire quarry referred to above; it came via London.— Ibid. , 121.

[244] Apparently about 440 tons.— Ibid.

[245] Pipe R., 16 Edw. III.

[246] The term 'damlade,' of uncertain meaning, seems to be peculiar to Yorkshire. See Fabric R. of York.

[247] Pipe R., 7 Edw. III.

[248] Misc. Bks., Tr. of R., 4, f. 142.

[249] Exch. K. R. Accts., 476, no. 5.

[250] Ibid., 461, no. 11.

[251] Exch. K. R. Accts., no. 12.

[252] V. C. H. Northants. , ii. 296-7.

[253] A similar method of splitting was employed in the case of the slates of Stonesfield, in Oxfordshire.— V. C. H. Oxon. , ii. 267.

[254] Ibid.; V. C. H. Northants. , ii. 296.

[255] V. C. H. Sussex, ii. 230.

[256] Exch. K. R. Accts., 476, no. 5.

[257] Ibid., 494, no. 4.

[258] Pipe R., 7 Edw. III.

[259] Exch. K. R. Accts., 502, no. 3.

[260] Fabric R. of York, 19.

[261] A fifteenth-century account for Launceston mentions the purchase of 'An iron tool for breaking stones in the quarry, called a polax, weighing 16½ lbs. , and two new wedges weighing 10 lbs.'—Exch. K. R. Accts., 461, no. 13.

[262] For a fuller history of the Purbeck marble quarries, see V. C. H. Dorset, ii. 331-8, from which the details given below are taken when other references are not given.

[263] See articles on 'Medieval Figure Sculpture in England,' Architectural Review, 1903.

[264] Liberate R., K. R., 37 Hen. III., m. 13.

[265] Exch. K. R. Accts., 467, no. 6 (2).

[266] Ibid., 469, no. 8.

[267] Ibid., no. 12.

[268] Arch. Journ., x. 116.

[269] Arch. Journ., lxi. 221-40.

[270] See e.g., the Flawford and Breadsall figures, ibid.; and the catalogue of Alabaster carvings exhibited at the Society of Antiquaries in 1910.

[271] Pipe R., 41 Edw. III.

[272] Arch. Journ. , lxiv. 32.

[273] Ibid., lxi. 229.

[274] The numerous cases of the export of alabaster carvings from Poole make it probable that the Purbeck carvers, when the demand for their marble fell off, worked the alabaster which exists in the district.— V. C. H. Dorset , ii.

[275] Some of these no doubt were sold at the time of the Reformation.—Arch. Journ. , lxi. 239.

[276] Ibid., 237-8.

[277] Ibid., 230.

[278] Arch. Journ. , lxi. 234-5.

[279] For an account of these, see Mr. Hope's article in Archaeologia, xli.

[280] Arch. Journ. , lxiv. 239.

[281] Ibid., x. 120.

[282] Fabric R. of York, 74, 78, 84, 90, 106.

[283] Fabric R. of York, 15.

[284] Exch. K. R. Accts., 504, no. 4.

[285] Hundred R., ii. 56.

[286] Exch. K. R. Accts., 467, no. 4.

[287] Customs Accts., 124/30.

[288] Probably chalk may be taken at about 4d. the quarter.

[289] Brit. Arch. Ass. Journal, lx.
[290] V. C. H. Sussex, ii. 231.
[291] Chaffers, Gilda Aurifabrorum, 19.
[292] Ibid., 23-5.
[293] A long chronological list of English goldsmiths is given by Chaffers, op. cit.
[294] Beverley Chapter Act Book (Surtees Soc.), ii., p. lxv.
[295] Cal. of City of London Letter Books, A., p. 180.
[296] Riley, Mems. of London , 350.
[297] Foreign R., 4 Hen. V., m. A.
[298] Camden Soc., xxxvii. 42.
[299] Chaffers, Gilda Aurifabrorum, 38.
[300] Ibid., 8, 9.
[301] Foreign R., 3 Hen. IV., m. E.
[302] Church Bells of England, by H. B. Walters, published since this was in print, contains much valuable matter.
[303] Chron. Battle Abbey (ed. Lower), 17.
[304] Cott. MS. Vesp. A., 22, f. 88.
[305] Stahlschmidt, London Bell-founders, 72.
[306] Ibid., p. 3.
[307] On the other hand, Fagniez (Docts. relatifs à l'histoire de l'Industrie, ii. 67) says that 'sainterius,' the title applied to Thomas de Claville who recast a bell for Notre Dame in 1397, is 'fait sur le vieux nom français des cloches saints ... qui se rattache à signa.'
[308] Ex. inf. Mr. C. H. Vellacott, from Assize Roll.
[309] Most of the London founders recorded by Mr. Stahlschmidt as known or possible bell- founders used the title 'potter.'— Loc. cit., 72-74.
[310] Early Chanc. Proc., 24, no. 138.
[311] Particulars are given in Raven, Bells of England, on which this account is based.
[312] To prevent the core, thickness, and cope sticking together, it seems to have been usual to dust them over with tan.
[313] Raven, op. cit., 74.
[314] V. C. H. Berks. , ii. 418.
[315] Raven, op. cit., 57.
[316] Early Chanc. Proc., 68, no. 144.
[317] Ch. Ward. Accts. St. Mary-at-Hill (E. E. T. S.).
[318] Raven, op. cit., 47.
[319] Ibid., 319.

[320] Recs. of St. Michael's. See also Ch. Wardens Accts. (Somerset Rec. Soc.).

[321] V. C. H. Berks. , ii. 416. Cf. H. B. Walters, Church Bells of England, ch. xii.

[322] Toulmin Smith, English Gilds, 295.

[323] Raven, op. cit., 69.

[324] London Bell-founders, 3.

[325] Ibid., 45.

[326] Issue R. of Exch., 239.

[327] Ibid., 346.

[328] Glouc. Corporation Recs.

[329] Sacrist Rolls of Ely, ii. 114, 138, where details of the outlay in the purchase of tin and copper, and of clay for the moulds and other necessaries are given.

[330] Raven, op. cit., 149.

[331] Ibid., 90.

[332] Fabric R. of York (Surtees Soc.), 9. Details are given.

[333] Raven, op. cit., where illustrations of the three panels are given.

[334] If the bell-shaped object is really the core, the ornamentation upon it must be ascribed to 'artist's licence,' as the surface of the core would in reality be quite plain.

[335] Inq. ad qd. damnum, File 108, no. 15.

[336] Exch. K. R. Accts., 462, no. 16. Amongst the items of expenditure are 'For eggs and ale bought for making the inscription round the bell 3d. For wax and cobbler's wax (code) for the same 5½d.' Possibly a mixture of eggs and ale was used to anoint the metal letter stamps and prevent their sticking to the clay of the cope.

[337] Early Chanc. Proc., 24, no. 138.

[338] De Banco, 831, m. 414; and Raven, op. cit., 164-6, quoting Year Book 9 Edw. IV., Easter Term, case 13.

[339] V. C. H. Shrops. , i. 47.

[340] Ryley, Mem. of London , 205.

[341] Enrolled Wardrobe Accts., no. 4.

[342] Enrolled Wardrobe Accts., no. 4.

[343] Foreign R., 9 Ric. II., m. A.

[344] Foreign R., 11 Ric. II., m. H.

[345] Issue R. of Exch., 346.

[346] Foreign R., 3 Hen. V., m. C.

[347] Foreign R., 3 Hen. IV., m. G.

[348] Ibid., m. I.
[349] Issue R. of Exch., 277.
[350] An illustration of a gun firing an arrow, drawn apparently in 1326, is mentioned in Proc. Soc. Ant. (xvi., 225), and at the battle of St. Albans in 1461 guns were used shooting 'arowes of an elle of length.'—Gregory's Chron. (Camd. Soc.), 213.
[351] Foreign R., 11 Ric. II., m. G.
[352] Foreign R., 3 Hen. V., m. C.
[353] Issue R. of Exch., 332.
[354] Ibid., 307-8.
[355] Foreign R., 3 Hen. V., m. C.
[356] In the Scottish expedition of 1496, five out of thirty-two 'faucons of brasse,' and twelve out of one hundred and eighty 'hakbusses of iren' were broken in action.—Exch. Tr. of R., Misc. Bks., 7, f. 140.
[357] Exch. Tr. of R., Misc. Bks., 8, f. 134.
[358] Early Chanc. Proc., 78, no. 81.
[359] Issue R. of Exch., 382.
[360] Foreign R., 12 Hen. VI., m. D.
[361] Figured in Suss. Arch. Coll., xlvi.
[362] He was paid at the rate of 16d. the hundredweight.—Exch. Tr. of R., Misc. Bks., 8, f. 139.
[363] Ibid., f. 34.
[364] Exch. Tr. of R., Misc. Bks., 8, f. 158.
[365] Early Chanc. Proc., 222, no. 112.
[366] Exch. Tr. of R., Misc. Bks., 8, f. 132.
[367] Ibid., f. 81.
[368] Ibid., f. 96.
[369] Early Chanc. Proc., 376, no. 32.
[370] Exch. Tr. of R., Misc. Bks., 8, f. 136.
[371] Ibid., f. 149.
[372] Exch. Tr. of R., Misc. Bks., vol. vii., passim , and L. and P. Hen. VIII., vol. i.
[373] Misc. Bks., vol. i., ff. 32, 78.
[374] Ibid., ff. 57, 61.
[375] Ibid., vol. iv., ff. 166, 181.
[376] See V. C. H. Sussex, ii. 246-9.
[377] Arch. Journ. , xxx. 319-24.
[378] See V. C. H. Northants. , i. 206-12.
[379] Ibid.

[380] Proc. Soc. Ant., xvi. 42.
[381] Brit. Arch. Ass. Journ. , xxxiii.
[382] Proc. Soc. Ant., xvii. 261-70.
[383] Somers. Arch. Soc., xiii. (2) 1.
[384] The dark colour of the Castor ware seems to have been caused by 'smothering' the kiln, by closing the vent, before the baking was complete.
[385] Misc. Accts. 1147, no. 23.
[386] Suss. Arch. Coll., xlv. 128-38.
[387] A Roman glazing kiln was found at Castor.— V. C. H. Northants. , i. 210.
[388] Fagniez, Docs. relatifs à l'histoire de l'industrie, no. 133.
[389] Dom. Bk., 65, 156, 168 b.
[390] e.g., 'Pottersfield' at Horsham, in which parish several finds of green glazed thirteenth- century vessels have been made.— V. C. H. Sussex , ii. 251.
[391] e.g., 'Geoffrey the potter,' who occurs in 1314 at Limpsfield, where remains of kilns have been found.— Proc. Soc. Ant. , iii.
[392] Lib. R., 51 Hen. III., m. 10. Simon 'le Pichermakere' of Cornwall is found in the fourteenth century sending his wares (presumably pitchers) to Sussex.—Anct. Pet., 10357-8.
[393] Inq. Nonarum , 361. Cf. the Hundred Rolls for Bucks.
[394] Mins. Accts., 507, no. 8227.
[395] V. C. H. Sussex, ii. 251.
[396] Ibid.
[397] Arch. Journ. , lix. 1-16.
[398] Proc. Soc. Ant., xv. 5-11.
[399] Rec. of Norwich, ii., no. 193.
[400] Riley, Mem. of London, 254.
[401] Ibid., 309. The monks of Boxley got as much as 10s. the thousand for some of the tiles from their tilery this year.—Mins. Accts., 1253, no. 13.
[402] Toulmin Smith, English Guilds, 399. At Lincoln, on the other hand, the tilers had formed a gild in 1346, and no tiler not belonging to the gild might stay in the town.— Ibid. , 184.
[403] V. C. H. Essex, ii. 456.
[404] Statutes, 17 Edw. IV.
[405] Thorold Rogers, Hist. of Agriculture and Prices, i. 490.
[406] Mins. Accts., 899, 900.

[407] Possibly from the French, fétu = a straw, from their being moulded as hollow cylinders.
[408] Turf was evidently used by the Cambridgeshire tilers for fuel.— Sacrist Rolls of Ely, ii. 67, 93, 137.
[409] 'Pro luto tredando ad dictos vj furnos pro tegulis inde faciendis.' The meaning of tredando is uncertain, but as the process is always mentioned after the clay had been carried to the kilns, it may have been the rolling of the clay to the right thickness for cutting tiles from.
[410] The words used for burning, or baking, the tiles are eleare and aneleare, both connected with our word 'anneal.'
[411] V. C. H. Sussex, ii. 251.
[412] In 1373 Peter at Gate leased the pasturage of Nackholt, where the tileries lay, at the low rent of 15s. on condition that he should serve as 'the lord's workman for making tiles.'
[413] V. C. H. Sussex, ii. 252.
[414] De Banco, 407, m. 12.
[415] Harl. Ch., 76 D., 32.
[416] Ibid., B. 50.
[417] Kelle = kiln: cf. Anct. D., A 4904, for a 'tylekelle' at Woolwich in 1450.
[418] Chron. de Melsa (Rolls Ser.), iii. 179-80.
[419] Hist. MSS. Com., Beverley MSS., 15.
[420] Ibid., 62.
[421] Sacrist R. of Ely, ii. 67.
[422] 'Flaunderistyle vocata Breke.'—Exch. K. R. Accts., 503, no. 12.
[423] Ibid., 472, no. 4.
[424] Hist. MSS. Com., Beverley MSS., 62.
[425] Hist. MSS. Com., Beverley MSS., 128.
[426] Ibid. , 47. These by-laws distinguish in one place between 'tilethakkers' and 'tile wallers,' the latter being what we should call bricklayers.
[427] Exch. K. R. Accts., 494, no. 4.
[428] Ibid., 467, no. 6 (6).
[429] Such were, no doubt, the paving tiles, of which 185,000 were bought from Richard Gregory, in 1357, for Westminster Chapel at 6s. 8d. the hundred.— Ibid. , 472, no. 4.
[430] Lethaby, Westminster Abbey, 48; Arch. Journal, lxix. 36-73.
[431] V. C. H. Derby, ii. 375. Ibid.
[432] V. C. H. Worces. , ii. 275.
[433] Suss. Arch. Coll., xi. 230.
[434] V. C. H. Surrey, ii. 295.

[435] John of London, 'glasyere,' and John, son of John Alemayn of Chiddingfold, were acquitted on a charge of burglary at Turwick in 1342.—Gaol Delivery R., 129, m. 12.

[436] Exch. K. R. Accts., 471, no. 6.

[437] V. C. H. Surrey, ii. 296.

[438] V. C. H. Surrey, ii. 296.

[439] In 1404 the Sacrist of Durham had in store 'of new coloured glass 2 scheff, of white glass and new 76 scheffe.'— Durham Acct. R. (Surtees Soc.), ii. 397.

[440] V. C. H. Surrey, ii. 297; V. C. H. Sussex, ii. 254.

[441] Exch. K. R. Accts., 471, no. 6.

[442] Durham Acct. R., ii. 393.

[443] Fabric R. of York, 76.

[444] Ibid., 83.

[445] Ibid., 37.

[446] Cat. of Pat., 1446-52, p. 255. The glorious windows now in King's College Chapel were made between 1515 and 1530 by four English and two Flemish glaziers, all of whom were resident in London.—Atkinson and Clark, Cambridge, 361.

[447] Fabric R. of York, 69.

[448] Ibid., 104, 108, 109.

[449] Hartshorne, Old Engl. Glass, 129.

[450] Ale is also said in one place to have been used 'pro congelacione vitri.'

[451] 'Frangentes et conjungentes vitrum super tabulas depictas.'

[452] The colours in some cases were fixed by heating, and it is presumably to this that an entry in an account of work at Guildford Castle in 1292 refers: 'In uno furno faciendo pro vytro comburendo—viijd.'—Exch. K. R. Accts., 492, no. 10.

[453] Pipe R., 2 Hen. II.

[454] V. C. H. Lincs. , ii. 302.

[455] See charter of Stephen, Cal. Chart. R., iii. 378.

[456] Pipe R., 19 Hen. II.

[457] Boldon Book.— V. C. H. Durham , i. 338.

[458] Printed by Riley, Liber Custumarum (i. 130-1), and, from an earlier copy, by Leach, Beverley Town Documents (Selden Soc.).

[459] The weavers were not villeins; had they been so, the leave of their lords would have been necessary before they could obtain the freedom of their town.

[460] Liber Custumarum, i. 33.

[461] Ibid., lxiii.
[462] e.g., Ashley, Economic History, i. 193: 'No cloth was manufactured for export; and a great part of the English demand for cloth'—indeed the whole of the demand for the finer qualities—'was met by importation.'
[463] Pipe R., 18 Hen. II.
[464] Pipe R., 27 Hen. II., and other years.
[465] Pipe R., 28 Hen. II.
[466] The 'list' is the strip of selvage at the edge of the cloth.
[467] Assize R., 358.
[468] Pat., 2 Hen. III., m. 4, 2.
[469] Pat., 9 Hen. III., m. 5.
[470] Lib. R., 30 Hen. III.: some years earlier cloth to be distributed at Worcester had been bought at Oxford.—Lib. R., 17 Hen. III.
[471] Lib. R., 35 Hen. III., m. 17.
[472] Liber Custumarum, i. 124.
[473] Cal. of S. P. Venice, i. 3.
[474] Lib. R., 36 Hen. III., m. 19.
[475] Arch. Journ. , ix. 70-1.
[476] The manufacture of this cloth must have originated in the village of Worsted, possibly with some settlement of Flemish weavers, but soon spread throughout the county.
[477] Rec. of Norwich, ii. 406.
[478] Statutes, 20 Hen. VI.
[479] Rot. Parl. iv. 230, 236.
[480] Customs Accts., 5, no. 7.
[481] Black Book of Admiralty (Rolls Ser.), ii. 197. Blues of Beverley, scarlets and greens of Lincoln, scarlets and blues of Stamford, coverlets of Winchester and cloth of Totness occur in wardrobe accounts of 1236. Pipe R., 19, 20 Henry III.
[482] Black Book of Admiralty (Rolls Ser.), ii. 187, 197.
[483] There was an 'omanseterowe' in the Drapery at Norwich as early as 1288.— Rec. of Norwich , ii. 8.
[484] Little Red Book of Bristol, ii. 4, 40. Narrow 'Osetes' were also made at Salisbury.—Exch. K. R. Accts., 344, no. 34.
[485] Liber Custumarum, i. 125; ii. 549.
[486] At Northampton the cloth trade, which in the time of Henry III. employed 300 men, had almost died out in 1334.— Rot. Parl., ii. 85.
[487] Liber Custumarum, i. 424.

[488] As early as 1331 special protection was granted to John Kempe of Flanders and any other clothworkers who wished to settle in England.— Pat., 5 Edw. III. , p. 2, m. 25.

[489] Statutes, 11 Edw. III.

[490] Rot. Parl., ii. 449, Close 13 Edw. III. , p. 3, m. 11.

[491] Little Red Book of Bristol, ii. 3.

[492] Langland, Piers Plowman.

[493] 'A Concise Poem on ... Shepton Mallet,' by Richd. Watts; printed in The Young Man's Looking Glass, 1641. With this may be compared Deloney's Pleasant History of John Winchcombe (Jack of Newbury), written some fifty years earlier.— V. C. H. Berks. , i. 388-9.

[494] 'Then to another room came they Where children were, in poor array, and every one sat picking wool, the finest from the coarse to pull.'

[495] 'Two hundred men, the truth is so, Wrought in their looms, all in a row; By every one a pretty boy Sat making quills with mickle joy.'

[496] The burler's business was to remove knots, loose ends and other impurities.

[497] The manufacture of these cloths was licensed in 1390, provided the quality was not improved.— Statutes , 13 Ric. II.

[498] Assize R.

[499] Liber Custumarum, ii. 549. Spanish wool is prominent amongst the imports at Southampton in 1310.—Customs Accts., 136, no. 8, n.

[500] Statutes, 4 Edw. IV.

[501] Statutes, 7 Edw. IV.

[502] An alkali, known as 'cineres,' possibly a kind of barilla or carbonate of soda (Rec. of City of Norwich, ii. 209) occurs fairly often: e.g., taxation of Colchester, Rot. Parl., i. 244.

[503] Little Red Book of Bristol, ii. 6.

[504] e.g., Customs Accts., 136/4, 136/12.

[505] Recs. of City of Norwich, ii. 209.

[506] Little Red Book of Bristol, ii. 16-22.

[507] Lands. MS., 121, no. 21.

[508] Cf. Rec. Borough of Northampton, i. 121: the compiler has mistaken 'wode' for wood.

[509] Little Red Book of Bristol, ii. 39.

[510] Little Red Book of Bristol, ii. 81-90.

[511] Rot. Parl., iv. 75.

[512] Early Chanc. Proc., 7, no. 23.

[513] Exch. K. R. Accts., 345, no. 16.

[514] Plunket appears to have been a pale blue, half the quantity of woad sufficing for plunkets that was used for azures, which in turn took half the amount required for blues.— V. C. H. Suffolk , ii. 258.

[515] Liber Custumarum, i. 129.

[516] There were no doubt the 'browne blewes' of later records: e.g., a Benenden clothier was fined in 1563 for 'a browne blewe, being a deceiptfull color.'—Memo. K. R., 7 Eliz., Hil., m. 330.

[517] Liber Custumarum, i. 125.

[518] Alkermes, an insect resembling cochineal.

[519] Statutes, 24 Hen. VIII.; cf. 4 Edw. IV.

[520] Little Red Book of Bristol, ii. 8, 9.

[521] Rec. of City of Norwich, ii. 119.

[522] Statutes, 4 Edw. IV. ; 3 Hen. VIII.

[523] V. C. H. Essex, ii. 255.

[524] V. C. H. Worcs. , ii. 286.

[525] V. C. H. Essex, ii. 383-4.

[526] The use of woof in place of warp was strictly forbidden.— Liber Custumarum , i. 125; Little Red Book of Bristol , ii. 2. At Worcester in 1497 any one bringing yarn to be spun into cloth was to bring the warp and the woof separate.— V. C. H. Worcs. , ii. 285.

[527] Rec. of City of Norwich, ii. 378.

[528] Rot. Parl., iii. 618.

[529] Arch. Journal, ix. 70: cf. Assize R., 787, m. 86.

[530] V. C. H. Notts. , ii. 345.

[531] Little Red Book of Bristol, ii. 4.

[532] Liber Custumarum, i. 134.

[533] Arch. Journ. , ix. 71.

[534] The suspension of worsted weaving for a month from 15 August was enforced in 1511 to avoid a shortage of agricultural labour during harvest.— Rec. of City of Norwich , ii. 376.

[535] Liber Custumarum, i. 423.

[536] Ibid. Candlewick Street (now Cannon Street) was the centre of manufacture of a coarse cheap cloth used for horse trappings, and also bought in large quantities for the King's almoner from 1330 to 1380.— Enrolled Wardrobe Accts., L. T. R., 2-4.

[537] Little Red Book of Bristol, ii. 40, 123.

[538] Statutes, 8 Hen. VI.

[539] V. C. H. Shrops. , i. 428.

[540] Statutes, 3 and 5 Henry VIII.

[541] Toulmin Smith, Engl. Gilds, 179. The gild was founded in 1297, but this regulation was probably of later date.
[542] Little Red Book of Bristol, ii. 127.
[543] Liber Custumarum, i. 128-9.
[544] Little Red Book of Bristol, ii. 13.
[545] Ibid., 79.
[546] V. C. H. Notts., ii. 346.
[547] V. C. H. Surrey, ii. 279.
[548] e.g., at Nottingham; V. C. H. Notts. , ii. 346.
[549] V. C. H. Warw. , ii. 252.
[550] Ibid.
[551] Statutes, 15 Ric. II.
[552] e.g., V. C. H. Surrey, ii. 344; V. C. H. Sussex, ii. 257.
[553] Exch. Dep. by Com., 41 Eliz., East. 1.
[554] Rot. Parl., i. 243.
[555] Statutes, 4 Edw. IV.
[556] V. C. H. Suffolk, ii. 262.
[557] Exch. K. R. Accts., bdles. 339-345.
[558] Marcus le Fair of Winchester was the only clothier not a Londoner from whom cloth was bought for the royal household in 1408.—Exch. K. R. Accts., 405, no. 22.
[559] V. C. H. Berks., i. 388.
[560] V. C. H. Suffolk, ii. 256.
[561] Hist. MSS. Com., Rep. viii. 93.
[562] Vlnage, or aulnage, from aulne = an ell.
[563] Statutes, 2 Edw. III.
[564] The penalty of forfeiture was withdrawn in 1354 as injurious to trade, deficient cloths being marked with their actual size.— Ibid. , 27 Edw. III.
[565] Statutes, 7, 8, 10 Hen. IV.
[566] Statutes, 11 Hen. VI.
[567] Rec. of City of Norwich, ii. 407.
[568] Rot. Parl., i. 292.
[569] Statutes, 13 Ric. II.; 11 Hen. IV.
[570] Rot. Parl., iii. 637.
[571] Statutes, 20 Hen. VI.
[572] Statutes, 4 Edw. IV.
[573] Statutes, 18 Hen. VI.
[574] Exch. Dep. by Com., 41 Eliz.

[575] Statutes, 5 Edw. VI. , 1 Mary, etc.
[576] See Memoranda Rolls, K. R., passim.
[577] Memo. R., K. R., Hil. 7 Eliz., m. 329. As an earlier instance, sixteen drapers in Coventry, thirteen in York, and seven in Lincoln, besides others elsewhere, were fined in the first quarter of 1390 for cloths of ray, not of assize.— Ibid. , Hil. 13 Ric. II.
[578] Exch. Dep. by Com., 30 Eliz., Hil., 8.
[579] Statutes, 14-15 Hen. VIII.
[580] Early Chanc. Proc., 141, no. 4.
[581] Statutes, 5 Hen. VIII.
[582] Rot. Parl., i. 292.
[583] The same material was used in 1323 for the pillows of the king's new beds.—Enr. Ward. Accts., 3, m. 2.
[584] Ibid., m. 10.
[585] Ibid., 2, m. 11.
[586] Engl. Hist. Rev., xvi. 289.
[587] Rot. Parl., ii. 347.
[588] Statutes, 4 Edw. IV.
[589] V. C. H. Surrey, ii. 343.
[590] Ibid., 343.
[591] Exch. K. R. Accts., 344, no. 10. The output from Berks. for the same period was 1747 kerseys, of which Steventon accounted for 574 and East and West Hendred for 520.— Ibid., 343, no. 24.
[592] Early Chanc. Proc., 140, no. 54.
[593] Statutes, 14-15 Hen. VIII.
[594] Rot. Parl., iv. 361.
[595] Enr. Ward. Accts., 4, m. 3.
[596] V. C. H. Worcs., ii. 284.
[597] V. C. H. Essex, ii. 384.
[598] Hist. MSS. Com., Rep. viii. 93.
[599] Rot. Parl., ii. 278.
[600] Exch. K. R. Accts., 405, no. 22.
[601] Rot. Parl., ii. 372.
[602] Enr. Ward. Accts., 5.
[603] Memo. R., K. R., 21 Eliz., East., m. 106.
[604] Rep. Dep. Keeper of Recs., xxxviii. 444; suit re draperies at Norwich, 1601.
[605] Thorold Rogers, Six Centuries of Work and Wages, 46.

[606] The suggestion that this law caused the trade to be established in Norwich (Recs. of Norwich, II. xii.) can hardly be correct, as there was no forest in Norfolk.

[607] For instances of the infringement of these and other regulations, see V. C. H. Surrey, ii. 331-5; V. C. H. Sussex, ii. 259.

[608] Lansd. MS., 74, 55.

[609] V. C. H. Oxon., ii. 254.

[610] V. C. H. Essex, ii. 459.

[611] V. C. H. Shrops. , i. 433.

[612] Rot. Parl., i. 243-65.

[613] Cott. MS. Vitell., C. vi., f. 239.

[614] Lansd. MS., 74, f. 52.

[615] Add. Chart. 30687.

[616] e.g., at Colchester in 1425.— V. C. H. Essex , ii. 459; and at Richmond in 1280.—Assize R., 1064, m. 32. In London the tanners were held partly responsible for blocking the course of the Fleet in 1306.— Rot. Parl., i. 200.

[617] Customs Accts., passim; e.g., those quoted in V. C. H. Dorset, ii. 327.

[618] Little Red Book of Bristol, ii. 114.

[619] The use of train oil instead of tallow was forbidden.

[620] V. C. H. Northants. , ii. 311.

[621] Riley, Mems. of London , 421.

[622] Lansd. MS., 74, f. 48.

[623] Lansd. MS., 74, f. 53.

[624] Riley, Mems. of London , 364-5.

[625] Ibid., 331.

[626] Ibid., 546-7.

[627] Lansd. MS., 74, f. 49.

[628] Ibid., 60.

[629] i.e., myrtle.

[630] Lansd. MS., 74, f. 53.

[631] Ibid., f. 48.

[632] Ibid., f. 58.

[633] At Colchester in 1425 the charge for tawing a horse hide was 14d., a buckskin 8d., doe 5d., and calf 2d.— V. C. H. Essex , ii. 459.

[634] Right Buffe were made from ‘Elke Skynnes or Iland hides brought out of Muscovia or from by Est’; the counterfeits were of horse, ox, and stag skins.—Lansd. MS., 74, f. 53.

[635] The price given for Spanish skins is probably an error; possibly the values of the 'right' and counterfeit' are reversed.
[636] In 1347 the London white tawyers charged 6s. 8d. for working a 'dyker [a packet of ten] of Scottes stagges or Irysshe,' and 10s. for the 'dyker of Spanysshe stagges.'—Riley, Mems. of London , 234.
[637] Corveiser was a still more common name for a shoemaker.
[638] Riley, Mems. of London , 572-3.
[639] Liber Albus, ii. 441-5.
[640] Riley, Mems. of London , 136.
[641] Ibid., 391.
[642] Little Red Book of Bristol, ii. 108.
[643] Little Red Book of Bristol, ii. 43.
[644] Ibid., ii. 105.
[645] Liber Albus, ii. 445.
[646] Riley, Mems. of London , 547.
[647] V. C. H. Northants. , ii. 318.
[648] Ibid.
[649] Liberate R., 50 Hen. III., n. 11.
[650] Pipe R., 31 Hen. I.
[651] Cal. Chart. R., ii. 34.
[652] A Dyetary of Helth (E. E. T. S.), 256.
[653] Giraldus Cambs. (Rolls Ser.), iv. 41.
[654] Mat. for Hist. of T. Becket (Rolls Ser.), iii. 30.
[655] Mon. Franc. (Rolls Ser.), ii. 8.
[656] Statutes, temp. Hen. III.
[657] '[A Brewer's assise] is xij d highing and xij d lowing in the price of a quarter Malte, and evermore shilling to q a '(= farthing).— Coventry Leet Bk. (E. E. T. S.), 397. In other words, ale was as many farthings a gallon as malt was shillings a quarter.
[658] Little Red Book of Bristol, 223.
[659] Assize R., 912, m. 49.
[660] Hundred R., ii. 216.
[661] Cal. Chart. R., i. 168.
[662] Ibid.
[663] V. C. H. Notts. , ii. 364.
[664] Coventry Leet Bk. (E. E. T. S.), 25, 678, 710.
[665] Ibid., 772.
[666] Beverley Town Docts. (Selden Soc.), liv. In 1413, 260 barrels (30 gallons) and firkins (7½ gallons) made for Richard Bartlot of

unseasoned wood and under size were burnt.—Riley, Mems. of London , 597.
[667] e.g., V. C. H. Sussex, ii. 261.
[668] Riley, Mems. of London , 319.
[669] From this it would seem that it was customary to put herbs into ale.
[670] Borough Customs (Selden Soc.), i. 185.
[671] Riley, Mems. of London , 386.
[672] Liber Albus, i. 360.
[673] V. C. H. Worcs. , ii. 256.
[674] Coventry Leet Bk. (E. E. T. S.). 675. There were at least thirty brewers in Oxford in 1380.— V. C. H. Oxon. , ii. 159.
[675] Riley, Mems. of London , 318.
[676] Andrew Borde, Introduction (E. E. T. S.), 123.
[677] Op. cit., 122.
[678] e.g., V. C. H. Sussex, ii. 262.
[679] Riley, Mems. of London , 225.
[680] Little Red Book of Bristol, ii. 229.
[681] Coventry Leet Bk. (E. E. T. S.), 584.
[682] V. C. H. Oxon., ii. 260.
[683] Liber Albus, i. 358.
[684] Coventry Leet Bk. (E. E. T. S.), 25.
[685] Suss. Arch. Coll., vii. 96.
[686] Liber Albus, i. 359.
[687] Coventry Leet Bk. (E. E. T. S.), 637.
[688] V. C. H. Oxon., ii. 260.
[689] Exch. Dep. by Com., Mich. 18-19, Eliz., no. 10.
[690] Cott. MS. Vesp., A. 22, f. 115.
[691] Recs. of Norwich, ii. 98.
[692] V. C. H. Sussex, ii. 261.
[693] Dyetary (E. E. T. S.), 256.
[694] Riley, Mems. of London , 666.
[695] V. C. H. Sussex, ii. 261.
[696] V. C. H. Dorset, ii. 367.
[697] Coram Rege 852, m. 23.
[698] Recs. of Norwich, ii. 100.
[699] V. C. H. Shrops. , ii. 422.
[700] V. C. H. Surrey, ii. 382.
[701] Ibid., 382-4.
[702] Dyetary (E. E. T. S.), 256.

[703] V. C. H. Dorset, ii. 369.
[704] Pipe R., 6 Hen. II. , Essex; 13 Hen. II., Windsor.
[705] Giraldus Cambr. (Rolls Ser.), iv. 41.
[706] Pipe R., 13 John.
[707] Mins. Accts., bdle. 899.
[708] V. C. H. Sussex, ii. 263.
[709] Ibid.
[710] Mins. Accts., 1128, no. 4.
[711] V. C. H. Sussex, ii. 263.
[712] Memo., K. R., 17 Ric. II., Hil.
[713] A Venetian Relation of the Island of England (Camden Soc.), 9.
[714] Statutes, 23 Edw. III.
[715] Six Centuries of Work and Wages, 233.
[716] Engl. Hist. Rev., xxi. 517.
[717] Assize R., 773.
[718] Statutes, 3 Edw. IV.
[719] Riley, Mems. of London , 163.
[720] Statutes, 13 Ric. II.
[721] Ibid., 15 Ric. II.
[722] Parly. Rolls, iii. 637.
[723] Statutes, 20 Hen. VI.
[724] Statutes, 4 Edw. IV.
[725] Unwin, Gilds of London, 139.
[726] Coventry Leet Bk. (E. E. T. S.), 32.
[727] Norwich Recs., ii. 278-310.
[728] Statutes, 28 Edw. III. Is iron raw material? Much labour has been expended on it before it reaches the market—but the same would apply to corn.
[729] e.g., Riley, Mems. of London , 255.
[730] Statutes, 11 Hen. VI.
[731] Riley, Mems. of London , 308.
[732] For an exhaustive examination of all that concerns wages, see the works of Professor Thorold Rogers.
[733] From the end of the fifteenth century the gradation of payments to workmen becomes more pronounced, marking the institution of the modern system.
[734] In the case of carpenters, etc., employed in country districts there appear to have been considerable variations.
[735] Exch. K. R. Accts., 472, no. 4.

[736] Beverley Town Docts. (Selden Soc.), 50.
[737] Statutes, 11 Hen. VII.
[738] Riley, Mems. of London , 538.
[739] Coventry Leet Bk., 574.
[740] Ibid., 673.
[741] Riley, Mems. of London , 253.
[742] Little Red Book of Bristol, 15.
[743] Exch. K. R. Accts., 467, no. 7.
[744] Norwich Recs., ii. 104.
[745] Riley, Mems. of London , 513.
[746] Coventry Leet Bk. (E. E. T. S.), 185.
[747] Riley, Mems. of London , 227.
[748] Little Red Book of Bristol, ii. 168.
[749] Liber Cust. , i. 99.
[750] Exch. K. R. Accts., 467, no. 7.
[751] Riley, Mems. of London, 226, 243. It is exceptional to find that at Leicester in 1264 the weavers were allowed to work at night.— Borough Recs. of Leicester, i. 105.
[752] Ibid., 538.
[753] Borough Recs. of Leicester, i. 547.
[754] Ibid., 226.
[755] Little Red Book of Bristol, 98; Coventry Leet Bk. , 302; Beverley MSS. (Hist. MSS. Com.), 47.
[756] Riley, Mems. of London , 532, 246.
[757] Ibid., 226, 239.
[758] Little Red Book of Bristol, ii. 4.
[759] Ibid., 97.
[760] Ibid., 30.
[761] Riley, Mems. of London , 573.
[762] Coventry Leet Bk. (E. E. T. S.), 638.
[763] For reproductions of some of the marks used by worsted weavers, see Norwich Recs., ii. 153.
[764] See the maps of medieval Bruges, Paris, and London in Unwin's Gilds of London, 32-4.
[765] Riley, Mems. of London , 392.
[766] Little Red Book of Bristol, ii. 182.
[767] Norwich Recs., ii. 237.
[768] Cf. Blackwell Hall in London, the sole market for 'foreign' cloth.— Riley, Mems. of London, 550.

[769] Liber Albus, ii. 444.
[770] Statutes, 37 Edw. III.
[771] Little Red Book of Bristol, ii. 117.
[772] Liber Cust., i. 118.
[773] Coventry Leet Bk. (E. E. T. S.), 180-3.
[774] The 'brakeman' reduced the bar iron to rods, ready to be drawn into wire.
[775] i.e., bending.
[776] i.e., girdlers; middle = waist.
[777] Little Red Book of Bristol, ii. 85.
[778] Toulmin Smith, English Gilds, 184.
[779] Ibid.
[780] Coventry Leet Bk. (E. E. T. S.), 27.
[781] Borough Recs. of Leicester, i. 105; Coventry Leet Bk., 95; Little Red Book of Bristol, ii. 7,8.
[782] Beverley Town Docts. (Selden Soc.), 53.
[783] Little Red Book of Bristol, 5.
[784] Ibid., 98.
[785] Early Chanc. Proc., 61, no. 478.
[786] Norwich Recs., ii. 289.
[787] e.g., Ibid., 199, 234; Woodruff, Hist. of Fordwich , 32-5.
[788] See e.g., Cal. of Pat. Rolls 1419-36, 537-88.
[789] Riley, Mems. of London , 346.
[790] Liber Cust., i. 423.
[791] Liber Cust., i. 423.
[792] A servant engaged by the year.— Little Red Book of Bristol , ii. 43.
[793] Coventry Leet Bk., 573.
[794] Little Red Book of Bristol, ii. 106.
[795] Toulmin Smith, English Gilds, 179.
[796] Riley, Mems. of London , 278.
[797] Little Red Book of Bristol, ii. 127.
[798] Riley, Mems. of London , 549.
[799] Ibid., 234.
[800] Ibid., 244.
[801] Little Red Book of Bristol, ii. 84.
[802] Early Chanc. Proc., 19, no. 491.
[803] Coventry Leet Bk. (E. E. T. S.), 560-1.
[804] e.g., Norwich Recs., ii. 290; Little Red Book of Bristol, ii. 125.

[805] Early Chanc. Proc., 66, no. 244.
[806] Coventry Leet Bk. (E. E. T. S.), 672.
[807] Early Chanc. Proc., 66, no. 244.
[808] Ibid., 38, no. 40.
[809] An ordinance of the fullers in 1418 forbade any master to take a stranger to serve him by covenant for more than fifteen days unless he engaged him for a whole year.— Little Red Book of Bristol , ii. 142.
[810] In the case of the London founders an intending journeyman had to satisfy the masters of his skill; if he could not, he must either become an apprentice or abandon the craft.—Riley, Mems. of London , 514.
[811] They had to give, and were entitled to receive, eight days' notice.—Coventry Leet Bk. (E. E. T. S.), 573.
[812] Coventry Leet Bk. (E. E. T. S.), 185.
[813] Liber Albus, ii. 444.
[814] Little Red Book of Bristol, ii. 106; Norwich Recs., ii. 104; Coventry Leet Bk. (E. E. T. S.), 656.
[815] Coventry Leet Bk. (E. E. T. S.), 786.
[816] Riley, Mems. of London, 495.
[817] Ibid., 542.
[818] Riley, Mems. of London , 609-12.
[819] Ibid., 653.
[820] Hist. MSS. Com. Coventry, 117-18.
[821] Coventry Leet Bk. (E. E. T. S.), 694.
[822] Coventry Leet Bk. (E. E. T. S.), 656.
[823] Ibid., 95.
[824] Little Red Book of Bristol, ii. 151.
[825] Riley, Mems. of London , 248, 307; cf. Acts of P. C., 1542-7 , p. 367.
[826] Riley, Mems. of London , 307, 514; Lambert, Two Thousand Years of Gild Life, 216.
[827] e.g., Little Red Book of Bristol, ii. 13.
[828] See the proceedings of the court of the tailors at Exeter.—Toulmin Smith, English Gilds, 299-321.
[829] Liber Cust. , i. 122; cf. Borough Recs. of Leicester, i. 89.
[830] Little Red Book of Bristol, ii. 14.
[831] Coventry Leet Bk. (E. E. T. S.), 302.
[832] Riley, Mems. of London , 232.
[833] Ibid., 281.
[834] Ibid., 293.
[835] Lambert, Two Thousand Years of Gild Life, 205.

[836] Toulmin Smith, English Gilds, passim.
[837] Norwich Recs., ii. 230.
[838] Makers of 'skeps,' or baskets.
[839] Norwich Recs., ii. 280-2.
[840] Norwich Recs., ii. 111.
[841] Ibid., 173.
[842] Sute, probably = course.
[843] Douset = a sweetmeat of cream, eggs, and sugar.

INDEX

C

D

E

F

G

H

I

J

K

L

M

N

O

P

Q

R

S

T

U

V

W

Y